Common Core Literacy Lesson Plans

Ready-to-Use Resources, K–5

Eye On Education
6 Depot Way West, Suite 106
Larchmont, NY 10538
(914) 833-0551
(914) 833-0761 fax
www.eyeoneducation.com

For information about permission to reproduce selections from this book, write:
Eye On Education, Permissions Department, Suite 106, 6 Depot Way West,
Larchmont, New York 10538

Library of Congress Cataloging-in-Publication Data

Common core literacy lesson plans : ready-to-use resources, K–5.
     p.   cm.
Includes bibliographical references.
ISBN 978-1-59667-223-9
1. Language arts (Elementary)—Curricula—United States.
I. Eye on Education (Firm)
LB1576.C5786 2013
372.6′ 044—dc23   2012030543

Contributing Writers: Lesli J. Favor, PhD, and Erin Schoenfeld
Sponsoring Editor: Robert Sickles
Production Editor: Lauren Davis
Copy Editor: Kathleen White
Designer and Compositor: Matthew Williams, click! Publishing Services
Cover Designer: Dave Strauss, 3FoldDesign

10 9 8 7 6 5 4 3 2 1

Also Available from Eye On Education

Common Core Literacy Lesson Plans:
Ready-to-Use Resources, 6–8
Ed. Lauren Davis

Common Core Literacy Lesson Plans:
Ready-to-Use Resources, 9–12
Ed. Lauren Davis

Vocabulary Strategies That Work:
Do This—Not That!
Lori G. Wilfong

Awakening Brilliance in the Writer's Workshop:
Using Notebooks, Mentor Texts, and the Writing Process
Lisa Morris

Teaching Grammar:
What Really Works
Amy Benjamin and Joan Berger

Teaching Critical Thinking:
Using Seminars for 21st Century Literacy
Terry Roberts and Laura Billings

Rigor Made Easy:
Getting Started
Barbara R. Blackburn

Rigor Is Not a Four-Letter Word
Barbara R. Blackburn

Math in Plain English:
Literacy Strategies for the Mathematics Classroom
Amy Benjamin

Students Taking Charge:
Inside the Learner-Active, Technology-Infused Classroom
Nancy Sulla

About the Editor

Lauren Davis, Senior Editor at Eye On Education, develops and edits books for teachers and school leaders on literacy and the Common Core State Standards. Lauren is a regular contributor to the Eye On Education blog and is the author of a bimonthly column called "Comments on the Common Core State Standards." She also presents on that topic. Recently, she was one of three judges for the Education World Community Lesson Plan Contest.

Prior to working for Eye On Education, Lauren served as senior editor of *Current Events*, a Weekly Reader classroom news magazine for students in grades 6–12. She also spent five years as director of language arts at Amsco School Publications, a publisher of workbooks and other resources for secondary students.

Lauren has a master's degree in English education from New York University. She began her career in the classroom, teaching 7th and 11th grade English in New York City. She also taught 6th grade English language arts in Westchester, New York. She is passionate about engaging students in learning.

Special Thanks

The editor would like to thank Lesli Favor and Erin Schoenfeld for their significant contributions to this book.

Lesli is a former English professor who now writes full-time for publishers of books for school classrooms and libraries. She is the author of 59 English/language arts texts, nonfiction books, and leveled readers.

Erin is a former elementary teacher who now provides literacy educational consulting for school publishers. This is the second book of lessons and literacy activities to which Erin has contributed.

Contents

Part 2: Writing

Part 3: Speaking and Listening

Part 4: Language

Handouts

Free Downloads

The handouts in this book are also available on Eye On Education's website as Adobe Acrobat files. Permission has been granted to purchasers of this book to download and print these handouts for free.

You can access the downloads by visiting Eye On Education's website: www.eyeoneducation .com. From the homepage, locate this book's product page by searching for the book title. Then click the link called "Log in to Access Supplemental Downloads" near the top of the page.

Your book-buyer access code is **CCL-7223-9**.

Note to Teachers

As your school switches over to the Common Core State Standards, you are likely wondering how your classroom will look different and how your lessons will change. Eye On Education is here to help. *Common Core Literacy Lesson Plans* provides a variety of engaging and easy-to-implement lesson plans based on the standards. You can teach these lessons as they appear, or you can modify them to fit your particular needs. The book also provides ideas for revamping your current lessons to make sure they meet the standards and for creating new lessons to meet additional standards.

These lesson plans emphasize rigorous texts, questions, and tasks, which are at the heart of the Common Core. They also stress authenticity and metacognition. Students need authentic assignments that reflect the kind of work they'll be asked to do beyond school doors. They also need to understand how they are learning so they can eventually do it on their own. Authenticity and metacognition increase engagement. When students become aware of their learning processes and see the value in what they're being assigned, they take more ownership in what they are doing and are more motivated to work hard.

How to Use This Book

This book is intended for grades K–5 teachers, literacy coaches, and curriculum leaders. The lessons can be used across the content areas; the standards emphasize the importance of literacy across the curriculum.

The lesson plans include reproducible handouts and links for further resources, and they can be extended from single lessons into full units (we provide ideas on how to do this). You can use each lesson as is, and you will learn how to create your own lessons based on these ideas. In that way, you will get a lot out of this book even when you are done teaching the lesson plans.

The book is organized by the strands of the Common Core State Standards—reading, writing, speaking and listening, and language. However, that sorting system indicates only the *main* emphasis for each lesson. In reality, each lesson incorporates more than one area. Reading, writing, speaking and listening, and language are integrated skills in the real world; they should be taught that way too.

Lesson plans are in order according to grade and skill level. Each lesson plan includes the following information:

- **Grade Level**—the main grade or grades for which the lesson is appropriate

- **Time Frame**—approximate number of class periods to complete the lesson. If you use the extension ideas, time frames will be longer.

- **Overview**—general information about the goal and focus of the lesson and how to adapt it to other grades if applicable

- **Common Core State Standards**—Most of the lessons cover more than one standard because the standards are not meant to be taught in isolation. Note that we listed the standards the main lesson covers, but if you choose to extend the lesson based on the suggestions provided, you will incorporate even more standards.

- **Objectives**—what students will learn

- **Background Knowledge Required**—what students need to know before delving into the lesson

- **Materials Needed**—texts and other materials to have on hand for the lesson

- **Agenda**—detailed, step-by-step instructions for the lesson

- **Differentiation**—ideas to adapt the lesson for struggling and advanced learners

- **Assessment**—assessment ideas, including rubrics and scoring guides

- **Notes**—a place for you to reflect on what worked with the lesson and what you would change the next time

Reading

Overview

The Common Core State Standards require using more-complex texts for teaching literacy. However, that doesn't mean students can't also read fun books at their own levels. The key is variety. Students should read some challenging texts so they learn to ponder words and meaning and reread when necessary. Students should also read some more accessible, self-selected texts that will help them develop fluency and a joy in reading. To teach the reading standards, you don't have to toss all your great lessons and start from scratch. Instead, you can look at your curriculum, evaluate the levels of the books you teach, and swap some for more challenging texts if necessary. You also need to add informational lessons to the mix, if you haven't been doing so already. The standards call for a balance of 50 literary texts and 50 informational (science and historical) texts. Informational texts should be included not just to present students with a new structure but also to help students build content-area knowledge. Consider a variety of topics when choosing informational texts. Finally, don't forget to include foundational reading skills in your reading lessons. There has been an educational shift away from phonics for some time, but the Common Core is reemphasizing the importance of phonics. You can incorporate mini-lessons on phonics, word recognition, and fluency into your reading units. For more tips to keep in mind when revising your lessons or creating new lessons, read the checklist below.

Planning Checklist

When planning a CCSS-based reading lesson, keep the following tips in mind:

☐ **Increase text complexity.** When selecting complex texts, consider quantitative and qualitative measures, and match readers to texts and tasks. Quantitative measures include word length and sentence length (often calculated using a readability scale such as the Lexile). Qualitative measures include the kinds of things a formula can't tell you, such as how well a text is written and whether it has layers of meaning (such as satire). Matching readers to texts and tasks means thinking about whether there is background knowledge required to understand a text, whether your students have this knowledge, whether they will find the material engaging, and so on. Consider all these factors when choosing complex texts. Don't rely solely on Lexiles, which are imperfect. A case in point:

on the Lexile scale, Hemingway's *The Grapes of Wrath* comes in at a grade 2 reading level, but you would never teach it to second graders because readers need more sophisticated mindsets to comprehend his ideas. Use your own judgment and your knowledge of your students along with Lexiles.

☐ Allow time for recreational reading too. David Coleman and Susan Pimentel, the authors of the standards, remind teachers that reading materials "will need to include texts at students' own reading level as well as texts with complexity levels that will challenge and motivate students" (p. 7). Students need opportunities to build their confidence as readers and their love of reading and to get into the habit of reading regularly. Giving students some books that they can get through quickly and be excited about will help accomplish that goal.

☐ Teach foundational skills such as spelling and sound patterns. According to the CCSS, teachers need to teach patterns and assess whether students are able to apply those patterns to new words. The goal is to teach skills students can use to become independent readers. The foundational skills included in the standards are print concepts (organization and basic features of print), phonological awareness (spoken words, syllables, and sounds), phonics and word recognition (phonics and word analysis to decode words), and fluency (read with accuracy, purpose, understanding; adjust rate, etc.). On pages 17–22 of the Common Core State Standards, Appendix A, you'll find detailed information about teaching these skills. The reading lesson plans in this book contain foundational skills mini-lessons to show you how to incorporate these skills into your lessons.

☐ Don't just read to students and have them read silently; make sure they have opportunities to read aloud. Give students plenty of opportunities to read texts at different levels and in different settings (e.g., to the teacher, with a partner, etc.). Assess students' accuracy, rate, and expression while reading.

☐ Teach students to do close readings of a text, and show them that it's OK to reread passages they don't understand. Model the kinds of things real readers do, such as rereading or asking themselves questions while reading. Use think alouds to show how you question a difficult text as you read. You may want to include some short, challenging texts so students can reread them several times. Also include some longer texts so students can build stamina.

☐ Use text sets so students can broaden their perspectives and deepen their understanding of a topic. For example, if you are teaching *The Hungry Caterpillar*, you might have students read an interview with Eric Carle and discuss how he writes or how he comes up with ideas (Blackburn, 2012, p. 24).

☐ Ask text-based questions, and show students how to go back to the text for answers.

☐ Include prereading activities that help students with "words and concepts that are essential to a basic understanding and that students are not likely to know or be able to determine from context" (Coleman and Pimentel, 2012, p. 8). However, be careful of prereading activities that summarize the text or reveal the major themes or ideas of the text. Such activities may make it harder for students to discover ideas on their own.

☐ Hold class discussions about a text. Also have students write about the texts they read or hear. Writing will help students work through their own thoughts about a text (Coleman and Pimentel, 2012, p. 9).

☐ Teach students how to figure out the meanings of unknown words. Teach context clues, and help students understand when they can and can't use them. Sometimes, an author doesn't provide enough clues, and readers need to check word meanings in a dictionary.

☐ Use graphic organizers such as Venn diagrams, cause-effect flow charts, T-charts, time lines, and idea maps to help students analyze the information in a text and compare two texts.

☐ Incorporate academic vocabulary into your informational text lessons. For example, teach *bar graph, glossary, icon(s), index, subhead*, etc. This will help students learn the material and learn how to talk about the material in the future.

☐ When you teach text elements and visuals, ask students why an author would use a certain visual. In other words, it's not enough to understand the information in a graph (e.g., the graph shows that 75 percent of kids like chocolate ice cream). Instead, help students understand why the graph is included in the first place (as opposed to no visuals or other forms of visuals) and how it supports the information in the text.

☐ Teach students to look at the structure of a text—captions, subheads, etc.—and how that structure aids comprehension. Point out text features, but also allow students to discover features on their own.

☐ Make sure your read alouds are interactive. Ask students questions along the way, and model your own questions as you read. This will build students' literacy skills more than a straightforward oral reading of the text (Arechiga, 2012, p. 72).

☐ Include think alouds so students can see what you do when your understanding breaks down.

☐ Teach the different organizational methods an author might use (cause-effect, problem-solution, etc.) as well as the key words that help readers determine structure. For example, a time-order essay would include sequencing words such as *first, next*, etc.

☐ When students answer a question about a text, make sure they say how they got their answers. Ask, "How did you know that?" This will give students practice going back to the text for evidence.

Lesson Plans at a Glance

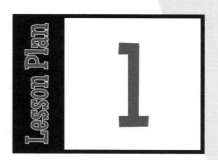

What's the Big Idea?

Identify the Main Topic and Details

Grade Level: K

Time Frame: Approximately one class period

Overview: This lesson uses an informational book, *Swirl by Swirl: Spirals in Nature,* to introduce and teach the concepts of main topic and details. You can use any short, simple informational book that you have in your classroom.

Common Core State Standards

- K: Reading, Informational Text, Standard 2: With prompting and support, identify the main topic and retell key details of a text.

- K: Reading, Informational Text, Standard 4: With prompting and support, ask and answer questions about unknown words in a text.

- K: Reading, Informational Text, Standard 5: Identify the front cover, back cover, and title page of a book.

- K: Speaking and Listening, Standard 2: Confirm understanding of a text read aloud or information presented orally or through other media by asking and answering questions about key details and requesting clarification if something is not understood.

- K: Language, Standard 6: Use words and phrases acquired through conversations, reading and being read to, and responding to texts.

Objectives

- Students will listen closely to an informational book read aloud.

- With guidance, students will identify the book's main topic.

- With guidance, students will talk about key details that connect to the main topic.

Background Knowledge Required

No particular background knowledge is required for this lesson.

Materials Needed

- A copy of *Swirl by Swirl: Spirals in Nature,* by Joyce Sidman, to read aloud

- Prepare a model art activity based on agenda item 5. Write a simple sentence about a spiral in nature (based on *Swirl by Swirl*), and draw a picture inspired by something in the book. For example, draw a snail with a spiral shell and write, "This snail has a spiral shell."

Agenda

1. **Introduction**: Introduce the book by saying something like, "I'm going to read a book to you. Let's look at the cover." (Show cover.) "Here it says that the title of the book is *Swirl by Swirl: Spirals in Nature.* Hmmm. Look at this picture clue on the cover." (Trace the spiral of the snail shell with your finger.). "What do you think a spiral is?"

2. **Read Aloud**: Read the book aloud. Pause at each page spread to help students identify spiral shapes. As you read, give emphasis to the words *spiral* and *swirl.* If an idea seems challenging, pause to think aloud: "It knows how to defend itself. Hmmm. What does it mean that a spiral can defend itself? The picture shows a sheep with spiral-shaped horns. These two sheep are butting horns. I see! These spiral-shaped horns must be very strong."

3. **Full-Class Discussion**: Guide students to identify the main topic of the book. Here is a suggested dialogue:

   "What an interesting book that was! Who can tell me what this book is mainly about? Well, *part* of the book is about sheep with curly horns. The sheep are on just two pages of the book. Let's figure out what the *whole* book is mainly about. Look at the cover. Let's read the title again. *Swirl by Swirl: Spirals in Nature.* Well, that is a big clue right there." (Write and say *swirl* and *spiral* on the board or chart paper, and draw a spiral shape.) "Yes, you are right! This whole book is about swirls, or spirals. The book's main topic is spirals. We know this because we read the title of the book. We also know this because we can read the pages of the book and look at the pictures. All the pages and all the pictures tell us something about spirals. The main topic is spirals."

4. **Full-Class Discussion**: Guide students to retell key details of the book. Here are some suggestions.

   "You know that the main topic of this book is spirals in nature." Point to the spiral you drew. "Who can tell me one thing about a spiral in nature? Listen to a few responses. To support each speaker, flip to the corresponding page in the book. Reinforce the answer by pointing out how the student has identified details in the book. "Sometimes we don't remember everything we read in a book. It's OK to read the book again or flip through the pages to jog our memories. Let's do that." Flip to a page spread that hasn't been discussed yet. "Here's a good page. What detail about spirals do we learn on these two pages? Let's read the words." Read the text. "Let's look at the picture clues." Point and think aloud or ask leading questions. "Good! That's right. You have told me about another detail in this book. This detail helps us understand the book's main topic, spirals in nature."

5. **Art Activity**: Show the model art activity that you prepared. Point out that you wrote a sentence that uses a capital letter and a period. Have students work

independently to write a sentence and draw a picture about a spiral in nature. If it's early in the year, have students dictate sentences to you. Later in the year, ask students to do their best to sound out (tap out) the words and spell as best they can.

6. **Wrap-Up**: Display the artwork in the classroom for a week. Each day, use one or more examples of student artwork to review the key concepts: "I'm looking at Ashlee's artwork here. What is this shape that she drew?" or "Cody wrote, 'The tornado is a spiral in nature.' Does his sentence help you remember the book that we read? What was the whole book mainly about?"

Extend the Lesson

- Examine the book's title page and back cover during the full-class discussion in agenda item 3, pointing out more word and picture clues to the book's main topic.

- Prepare an extended art activity in which each student makes a four-page book, with a cover, about spirals in nature. The books can be small, such as 3 inches by 7 inches, and students can cut out the pages on dotted lines that you arrange on larger sheets. Write a title on the covers: "My Book About Spirals, by _____ ." On each page, write a prompt for students to illustrate: "This animal has a spiral shape. This animal is a _____ ." "Here is the spiral shape that I like best." When they have completed their pages, staple them together as books. Review key concepts by asking, "What is the main topic of your book? What is it mostly about? What detail did you use to tell about the main topic? What does the cover of your book say? Who is the author of your book?"

Differentiation

For students who need extra support

- Pass out coloring sheets that are similar to the cover of *Swirl by Swirl*, showing a clear spiral in nature, such as a shell or snail. During the reading of the book, pause to ask students to trace the spiral on their coloring sheets with a finger. Ask them to say the word aloud with you. (In an ideal world, each student would have a copy of the book to hold, but this is not normally possible!)

- Give students a turn to come up and hold the book. Ask them to point to the title and read it aloud with you. Point to the word *Swirl* and say, "*Swirl*. This word is in the title. Do you think it is a clue to the book's main topic?" Read the title again. Ask, "What other word in the title is important? Do you think it is also a clue to the book's main topic? What is the book's main topic?"

For advanced students

- After reading the book, ask a few questions that are more complex. "What kind of spiral can happen in the weather?" (Answer: tornado) "Where can you find a spiral shape on a monkey?" (Answer: when it curls its tail around a branch)

Assessment

Use this rubric to evaluate the art activity. You can assign a grade based on points that a student earns, with 4 being a top score.

Points to Earn	Task
2	Writes a sentence about a spiral in nature.
0.5	Begins the sentence with a capital letter.
0.5	Ends the sentence with an end mark (e.g., period, exclamation point).
1	Draws a spiral shape that is connected to nature in some way.
Top Score: 4	

Additional Resources

ReadWorks has a three-lesson kindergarten unit on main idea and details: www
.readworks.org/lessons/gradek/main-idea.

Foundational Skills
Mini-Lesson

Onsets and Rimes of Single-Syllable Words

Common Core State Standards

K: Reading, Foundational Skills, Standard 2: Demonstrate understanding of spoken
words, syllables, and sounds (phonemes). c. Blend and segment onsets and rimes
of single-syllable spoken words. e. Add or substitute individual sounds (phonemes)
in simple, one-syllable words to make new words.

Planning and Preparation

Prepare a work sheet for students, as shown below. You can use the words listed
(the first word in each row is drawn from or inspired by *Swirl by Swirl*) or choose your
own single-syllable words. Make copies for students and yourself.

fit	_it	s
for	f_r	a
web	we_	t
sun	_un	f
red	_ed	b

Agenda

1. In a list, write five single-syllable words on the board in large letters. If using the
   work sheet above, write *fit, for, web, sun,* and *red*.

2. Tell students, "Here is a list of words that we will read today. Listen to me read them
   to you." Point to the onset (initial consonant sound) in *fit* and say *eff*. Pause briefly,

point to the rime (the vowel and the rest of the syllable), and say *it*. Pause briefly and then say the whole word: *fit*. Repeat the process of segmenting and then blending the onset and rime of each word in the list.

3. Tell students, "You know a lot about the alphabet. You know the sounds that letters make. You can read these words (point to list on board) by saying the sounds that the letters make. Let's practice reading these words together." Go through the list, repeating the process of segmenting and then blending the onset and rime of each word, pointing as you say each sound or word. Students should read aloud with you.

   Note: You could break the mini-lesson here and finish it on another day.

4. Distribute the work sheet. Tell students, "Look at the first row on this page (hold up work sheet and run finger across first row). Let's read the first word in this row." Read the onset and rime of *fit*, and then read the word as a whole. Tell students, "We can take out one letter of *fit* and put another letter in its place. This will make a new word. Let's do it together." Hold up the work sheet and point to _*it*. "We have a blank and then *it*. Let's take the *s* from over here at the side, and write the *s* in the blank here. Do that on your own paper. Write the *s* in the blank. Now let's say the new word together." Read the onset and rime of *sit*, and then read the word as a whole.

5. Repeat the process of making a new word out of each initial word. Depending on your students' familiarity with this process, you could choose to guide the class through the whole activity or ask them to work in small groups to complete the remaining four words.

Assessment

Meet one-on-one with students and have them read aloud the two words in each row of the work sheet. Use the opportunity to clarify sounds of letters or the concept of segmenting and then blending sounds to read a word.   ■

Notes

After implementing the lesson, make notes on what worked and what you would change next time.

_____

_____

_____

_____

Each One Is Different

Compare Two Books on the Same Topic

Grade Levels: K–1

Time Frame: Approximately one or two class periods

Overview: This lesson teaches students to recognize that books on the same topic can give different information on that topic. As model texts, the lesson uses two books about pumpkins. You can use this lesson (adapting the handout) with any two informational books on the same topic that you have in your classroom.

Common Core State Standards

- K: Reading, Informational Text, Standard 9: With prompting and support, identify basic similarities in and differences between two texts on the same topic (e.g., in illustrations, descriptions, or procedures).

- 1: Reading, Informational Text, Standard 9: Identify basic similarities in and differences between two texts on the same topic (e.g., in illustrations, descriptions, or procedures).

- K: Writing, Standard 2: Use a combination of drawing, dictating, and writing to compose informative/explanatory texts in which students name what they are writing about and supply some information about the topic.

- 1: Writing, Standard 2: Write informative/explanatory texts in which students name a topic, supply some facts about the topic, and provide some sense of closure.

Objectives

- Students will listen closely to two informational books on the same topic read aloud.

- With guidance, students will tell how pictures and information in the two books are alike and different.

- Students will make their own books and then compare and contrast their books in a small-group setting.

Background Knowledge Required

No particular background knowledge is required for this lesson.

Materials Needed

- Two informational texts on the same topic that have noticeable differences in illustrations, descriptions, or procedures. Suggested books are *From Seed to Pumpkin*, written by Wendy Pfeffer and illustrated by James Graham Hale, and *Pumpkins*, by Ken Robbins.

- Copies of the handout: Comparing Books Activity Sheet, p. 14. Note: Make two extra copies: one to show the class as you give instructions for the project and one to complete ahead of time so you can show the finished product as you give instructions.

Agenda

1. **Introduction**: Have a brief discussion with students about how two things can be alike in some ways but different in other ways. Provide some concrete examples. For example, refer to two teachers: "Mrs. A and Mrs. B are both women. This is one way they are *alike*. But Mrs. A has brown hair, and Mrs. B has black hair. This is one way they are *different*." You could use sandwiches, pizzas, dogs, or other familiar things to review the concepts of alike and different.

    Tell students that you are going to read two books to them. Both books are about pumpkins. This is one way they are alike. Hold up books to show covers. But the books are not *exactly* alike. Ask students to look at the covers and tell you one way that the books are different. For example, the covers have different pictures or one cover has a drawing, and the other cover has a photograph. Perhaps one cover has children on it, and the other cover doesn't.

2. **Read Aloud**: Read one of the books aloud, showing the pictures as you go along. Then tell students that now they will make some notes about the book. On the board or chart paper, create a blank T-chart. Write the title of the book at the top of the left side. Under that, write the word *pictures*. Ask students to tell you about the pictures. Are they drawings or photographs? What kinds of things do they show? Repeat the process with *descriptions* and *information* (or other categories you choose). It's OK if there is just one example per category right now. You can add more later.

    Read the other book aloud. Fill in the other half of the T-chart using information from this book. As you discuss the second book, students may recall examples from the first book to add to the chart. If they don't recall examples on their own, guide them in going back and forth between the books to make comparisons.

3. **Book-Making Activity**: Organize students into small groups. Show them the handout and the model pumpkin book, and explain that they will write, color, or draw on each page to complete their own books. Give instructions about cutting out and stapling the pages. Have students make their books.

4. **Wrap-Up**: In their small groups, have students compare and contrast the books they have made. Color choices, jack-o'-lantern faces, favorite things, etc. may be alike or different from book to book. Make sure students compare both words and pictures, with guidance if necessary.

Differentiation

For students who need extra support

- In the days leading up to this lesson, set out a display of pairs of books. Choose a range of wordless picture books, below-grade readers, and grade-level readers (with each pair falling at the same reading level). Give students time to read and examine the books on a couple of different occasions. Each time, make comments such as,

"Oh, I see you are looking at two books about baby chickens. This book shows how the baby hatches. The other book shows how the baby grows up."

For advanced students
- Add above-grade readers to the pairs of books (see the previous bullet). Instead of making declarative comments to these students, ask leading questions, such as "What are your two books about? Oh, they're about the same topic. Do these books tell you the exact same thing? Oh, they don't? What does this book tell that's not in the other book?"

Assessment

Before you begin the lesson (and before the differentiation activity, if included), make a list of students' names. As you do each part of the lesson or an activity, place tick marks next to the names of students who demonstrate understanding of comparing and contrasting text and pictures. The more participation showing understanding, the more ticks. Jot brief notes if necessary. Once the wrap-up activity is complete, check to see if any students have zero or just one or two ticks. If this is the case, schedule a reading group with these students and repeat the read aloud activity, this time using simpler texts.

Additional Resources

ReadWorks has compare-and-contrast lesson units (three lessons per unit) for kindergarten and first grade at www.readworks.org/lessons/gradek/compare-and-contrast. Use the menu in the sidebar to navigate to the first-grade lessons. Neither unit compares two books on the same topic, but you can adapt the ideas and activities to this objective.

Final *E* and Long Vowel Sounds

> **Foundational Skills Mini-Lesson**

Common Core State Standards

1: Reading, Foundational Skills, Standard 3: Know and apply grade-level phonics and word analysis skills in decoding words. c. Know final *e* and common vowel team conventions for representing long vowel sounds.

Planning and Preparation

In the top half of a sheet of paper, create a chart like the one that follows. Use large letters and large spaces for students to write in. In the lower half of the page, insert a large empty box. Write the instructions, "Draw a picture of one of the words." Make copies for the students.

1. man __ __ __	→	2. mane __ __ __ __
3. kit __ __ __	→	4. kite __ __ __ __
5. hop __ __ __	→	6. hope __ __ __ __
7. hug __ __ __	→	8. huge __ __ __ __

Agenda

1. Write the vowels on the board. Say, "Let's review our vowels. Read them with me: *a, e, i, o, u.* Good! When you read a word, the vowel helps you know how to say the word. Look at this word." Write *cap* on the board. "What vowel is used to spell this word? Right! *A.* Now, who can read this word for me? . . . Good! *Cap.*"

2. "Now watch this. I am going to add a vowel to the end of *cap.*" Write *e* to spell *cape.* "What letter did I add to the end of *cap*? Yes, I added an *e.* It is one of our vowels. Who can read this new word for me? Yes, that's right: *cape.*"

3. "What is strange about the *e* at the end of *cape*? We don't say its sound at all! It is completely quiet in this word. It is silent. Did you notice something else? When we put *e* at the end of *cap*, it makes a new word: *cape.* In the new word, the *a* makes a different sound." Point to the *a* in *cape,* and then cover the *e* in *cape.* "This was our first word. *Cap.* This word has a short *a* sound: *caaaap.*" Draw out the short *a* sound, and uncover the *e.* "This is our second word: *cape.* In this word, the *a* has a long *a* sound: *caaaape.* What is the only difference in how these words are spelled? Yes! The quiet *e. Cap* does not have a quiet *e,* but *cape* has a quiet *e.* When you see the quiet *e* at the end of a word, that is a signal. It is saying, 'Hey! Notice me! I am telling you to make a long vowel sound in this word!'"

4. Pass out the work sheet. Guide students in reading the letters in *man* aloud, reading the whole word and then writing the letters in the blank to spell the word. Taking the words in order, spell, read, and write each word as a class.

5. Have students choose one word from the page and draw a picture to show it.

Assessment

On another day, pass out copies of the top half of the work sheet. Review the key ideas of the lesson, and then have students complete the work sheet independently. Evaluate the work sheets, awarding a half point for each word spelled correctly (top score for writing: 4). Then meet one-on-one with students and have them read the words to you, awarding a half point for each word pronounced correctly (top score for reading: 4). ■

Notes

After implementing the lesson, make notes on what worked and what you would change next time.

_____

_____

_____

_____

Name: _____ Date: _____

Comparing Books Activity Sheet

My Book About Pumpkins

by _____

1. This is what a pumpkin looks like.

The color of a pumpkin is

_____ .

2. Pumpkins grow on vines.

The color of a vine is

_____ .

3. Some jack-o'-lanterns look happy.

Some jack-o'-lanterns look sad.

Some jack-o'-lanterns look scary.

My jack-o'-lantern looks

_____ .

4. My favorite thing about pumpkins is

_____

_____ .

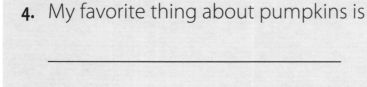

p u m p k i n

14

How Do I Find What I Need?

Identify and Use Text Features

Grade Levels: 1–3

Time Frame: Approximately one or two class periods

Overview: This hands-on lesson introduces grade-relevant text features, both print and digital, that help students find information efficiently. Students with greater exposure to a wide variety of books and access to the Internet at home are likely to be more familiar with a range of text features than students who have limited exposure. This lesson can be used alone or in conjunction with other reading or writing lessons to make sure that all students have the opportunity to master using grade-appropriate text features.

Common Core State Standards

- 1: Reading, Informational Text, Standard 5: Know and use various text features (e.g., headings, tables of contents, glossaries, electronic menus, icons) to locate key facts or information in a text.

- 2: Reading, Informational Text, Standard 5: Know and use various text features (e.g., captions, bold print, subheadings, glossaries, indexes, electronic menus, icons) to locate key facts or information in a text efficiently.

- 3: Reading, Informational Text, Standard 5: Use text features and search tools (e.g., keywords, sidebars, hyperlinks) to locate information relevant to a given topic efficiently.

- 1–3: Speaking and Listening, Standard 1: Participate in collaborative conversations with diverse partners about [*grade-level*] *topics and texts* with peers and adults in small and larger groups.

Objectives

- Students will identify common features of informational text, such as glossaries and electronic menus, and the purpose for using each one.

- Students will use common features of informational text.

- Students will work collaboratively in small groups to complete tasks and contribute ideas to full-class discussions.

Background Knowledge Required

Students should know the differences in purpose between texts that tell stories and texts that give information.

Materials Needed

- A dozen or so informational books, magazines, and color-printed webpages that use features relevant to your grade (see lists in standards). You may want to choose texts that relate to topics that students are studying in social studies, science, and math. In each book or printout, use a sticky note to flag a text feature that you would like students to examine.

- Copies of the handout: Text Features Activity Sheet, p. 20

    Note: This handout works well as a review of text features introduced in grades 1–3. You may want to use the handout as a model for creating a work sheet tailored to a lower grade or to the specific text features that you taught in your lesson.

Agenda

1. **Introduction**: Set up a display of the informational books, magazines, and printouts. Tell students that these are different types of informational texts. Hold up one of the texts, and open it to the sticky note so students can see a feature such as the table of contents, a picture with a caption, or a sidebar. Explain that informational texts often use text features to help readers find information easily. Demonstrate using a text feature, such as an index or electronic menu, to find a specific fact. On the board, write the term *text features* and the definition "parts of a book, magazine, or webpage that help people find information easily." Tell students that today, they will work with partners (or in small groups) to learn about and use different kinds of text features. If you think the repetitive use of *text features* is becoming noticeable, that's great! You want students to incorporate the term into their long-term academic vocabularies.

2. **Pairs (or Small Group) Activity**: Organize students into pairs or small groups. Each group should have one book, magazine, or printout from the display. Have each group complete part 1 of the handout with your guidance as you read aloud the directions, giving time to complete each item as you go.

3. **Academic Vocabulary**: Briefly identify and explain the types of text features that you have marked in the model texts (icon, heading, hyperlink, etc.). List the terms on the board. As you teach each term, ask students to say the term aloud with you.

    Note: You can break the lesson here and continue on another day.

4. **Shared Speaking**: Have each small group share its informational text and responses to part 1 of the handout with the full class. If you are short on time, ask just one group per type of text feature to share. To review the ideas another day, you can have the other groups share.

5. **Wrap-Up**: Read aloud the instructions for part 2 of the handout, and guide students as they write answers to each question independently.

Extend the Lesson

- Have students use a dictionary or an encyclopedia to look up the name of each text feature. They can do this in conjunction with the academic vocabulary discussion and/or wrap-up.

- Have students create posters to hang in the classroom. Each poster should name a text feature, tell why it is useful, and include a written or printed example of that feature.

- Have students bring in (from home or a library) a text that contains one of the features you studied. Have each student show the text feature to the class, identify it, and explain why it's useful.

- Use the lesson plan two or more times, each time focusing on just one type of text feature.

Differentiation

For students who need extra support

- In advance of the lesson, prepare posters like those described in the lesson extension activity, above. Review these posters during the academic vocabulary part of the lesson and, if needed, during the wrap-up. In lessons during the next week or so, make a point of asking volunteers to use a particular text feature to find information. Use the posters to help refresh and reinforce students' knowledge.

For advanced students

- Ask a student in each group to read aloud each question for the group to answer in part 1 of the activity. Indirectly, this establishes this student as the group leader, and he or she is in a position to answer questions or give further direction to the group.

Assessment

Check students' work on part 2 of the handout. For scoring purposes, there are 20 write-on blanks distributed among questions 6–15. You could use a 100-point scale to grade part 2, or you could use this rubric:

Score	The student
4	Uses at least eight of the nine text-feature terms correctly.
3	Uses at least six of the nine text-feature terms correctly.
2	Uses at least four of the nine text-feature terms correctly.
1	Uses at least two of the nine text-feature terms correctly.
0	Does not use any of the text-feature terms correctly.

Additional Resources

This short, grade-3 lesson plan includes a one-page magazine article and a work sheet and covers bold print, subheadings, captions, and sidebars: www.monet.k12.ca.us/curriculum/librarylessons/Lessons/3rd/3_Presidents_Place.pdf.

Consonant Digraphs

Common Core State Standards

1: Reading, Foundational Skills, Standard 3: Know and apply grade-level phonics and word analysis skills in decoding words. a. Know the spelling-sound correspondences for common consonant digraphs.

Planning and Preparation

- Working with a landscape-oriented layout, divide a sheet of paper into four columns. At the top of each column, write one of these headers: CH says, SH says, TH says, WH says. Make copies for the students and yourself.

- On one or more sheets of paper, create word cards that you can cut apart. Use these words or words you choose that include the digraphs listed above: *chant, chart, chin, sheep, ship, dish, the, path, thunder, whale, white, when.* Copy the pages (enough to have one set of word cards per small group of students), and cut the word cards apart, keeping the sets separate. However, mix up the cards in each set so that words with the same digraph are not all together.

Agenda

1. Remind students that the alphabet has two kinds of letters: vowels and consonants. Each letter has its own sound, but it can also work as a team with another letter to make a new sound. Write *C* on the board. Have students tell you what sounds *c* can make (soft or hard *c*, as in *cent* and *cake*). Write *H* on the board, and ask volunteers to tell you what sound it makes. Finally, write *CH* on the board. Tell students that these two letters work as a team to make the *ch* sound in *choo-choo.* Give other examples, such as *cheer, beach,* and *chirp.* Write each on the board, and have students say the words with you. Underline the digraph (*ch*) to emphasize that the two consonants work as a team to make one sound.

2. Organize students into small groups. Pass out a four-column work sheet to each student and a set of word cards to each group. In each group, students must say the word on each card and look and listen for the digraph. They should sort the cards into four piles to match the four headings on their work sheets (CH, SH, TH, WH). Finally, each student should copy the words into the appropriate column of his or her work sheet.

Assessment

Check students' work on the work sheet to see how many of the digraphs they sorted correctly. If the class is struggling, repeat the activity on another day. If individuals are struggling, have selected students repeat the activity in a small group with you as group leader while other students complete a different activity. ■

Notes

After implementing the lesson, make notes on what worked and what you would change next time.

_____

_____

_____

_____

Name: _____   Date: _____

Text Features Activity Sheet

Your teacher will read this page to you. Listen. Then, write your answers.

Part 1: Study the text feature that you or your group was given. Answer these questions.

1. What kind of text do you have? A book? A magazine? A print-out of a webpage? _____

2. What text feature are you looking at? _____

3. Where is the text feature located in the text? For example, is it in the front or back of the book? Is it at the side of a page? In a paragraph? _____

4. What kind of information does the text feature help you find? For example, does it help you find a word in the book? A chapter? Facts about what you see in a picture?

   _____

5. Look at the text feature. Give an example of the information that it gives to readers of this book, magazine, or webpage. For example, if you are looking at a glossary, write down one of the entries from the glossary.

   _____

   _____

   _____ .

Your teacher will read this page to you. Listen. Then, write your answers.

Part 2: Use text features to dream big! Write an answer to each prompt.

6. If I could write a book, it would be about _____ .

7. In the book's **table of contents**, I would include these three chapters:

- _____
- _____
- _____ .

8. Three of the **keywords** in my book would be

- _____
- _____
- _____ .

9. My book's **index** would include these three topics:

- _____
- _____
- _____ .

10. One of the **sidebars** in my book would tell about _____
_____ .

11. In my book, I would include a picture of _____ .

The **caption** would say _____ .

12. If I could make a webpage about my book, I would **title** the page _____ .
This would help people find my page on the Internet.

13. The main **menu** on my webpage would have these three words to click on:

- _____

- _____

- _____ .

14. One of the **icons** on my webpage would be a/an

_____ .

If a visitor clicked on the icon, this is what would happen:

_____ .

15. The visitors to my webpage might want to find other pages like mine. I would put a **hyperlink** on my webpage. It would take visitors to _____

_____ .

Paint a Picture With Your Words!

Describe a Character's Looks, Actions, and Feelings

Grade Level: 1; can be adapted to other grades (see note in Overview)

Time Frame: Approximately one class period

Overview: Students in grades 1–5 are asked to describe characters in a story. In first grade, the emphasis is on identifying key details in the text and illustrations to describe the characters. The complexity of character descriptions increases as students progress from grade to grade. Though this lesson was designed for first grade, you can adapt it to higher grades by selecting a more complex text to read aloud and by asking students to explain how a character's actions move the plot forward, for example, or to compare and contrast two characters.

Common Core State Standards
- 1: Reading, Literature, Standard 3: Describe characters, settings, and major events in a story, using key details.

- 1: Reading, Literature, Standard 7: Use illustrations and details in a story to describe its characters, settings, or events.

- 1: Language, Standard 5: With guidance and support from adults, demonstrate understanding of word relationships and nuances in word meanings. a. Sort words into categories . . . to gain a sense of the concepts the categories represent.

Objectives
- Students will use details and examples from a story to describe a character's looks, actions, and feelings.

- Students will use illustrations in a story to help describe a character's looks, actions, and feelings.

- Students will sort descriptive words and phrases into categories to better understand the concepts that the categories represent.

Background Knowledge Required
Students should be familiar with the term *character* from kindergarten, but this lesson reviews the term.

Materials Needed

- Copy of *Curious George's First Day of School*, to read aloud.

- Copies of the handout: Character Activity Sheet, p. 28

Agenda

1. **Introduction**: Tell students that today they are going to learn how to describe characters from stories. If necessary, remind students that a character is a person or an animal in a story. When they *describe* a character, they tell about his or her looks, actions, and feelings. On the board or an easel chart, draw a three-column chart. Label the columns Looks, Actions, and Feelings. Have a brief conversation with students in which you ask them to give you examples of a character and how he or she looks (e.g., Batman wears a mask and has big muscles), what he or she did once (e.g., Emily Elizabeth took Clifford the Big Red Dog to show and tell), and what he or she felt once (e.g., Henry was sad when his dog Mudge got lost). As students give examples, jot down keywords in the chart. Tell students that a chart such as this can help them sort their words and ideas into categories—in this case, the three categories of Looks, Actions, and Feelings.

2. **Modeling Activity**: Create a fresh three-column chart labeled Looks, Actions, Feelings. Read aloud pages 3–8 of *Curious George's First Day of School*. As you read each page or paragraph, pause to think aloud: "This story is about a character named George. I'll write George's name at the top of my chart. Here it says that George was excited. Excitement is a feeling. I will write the word *excited* in the chart under Feelings." Use picture clues to describe George. "In this picture, George is holding a book for the children. This is an action. I will write *held the book* under Actions."

3. **Full-Class Activity**: Read aloud pages 9–13 of the story. After each page, paragraph, or picture, pause to ask students what they can tell you about George's looks, actions, and feelings. Continue to fill in the three-column chart.

4. **Independent Activity**: Pass out copies of the handout. Explain that it is a chart like the one the students have been creating as a class. Ask them to write the character's name (George) at the top of their charts. Point out that the names of the columns are Looks, Actions, and Feelings. Read the examples of words that could describe looks, actions, and feelings. Tell students that they will fill in their charts as you read the rest of the story. Read the rest of the story aloud, pausing to guide students in identifying George's looks, actions, and feelings. It's OK if a student writes something such as *looks sad* in the Looks column (as opposed to the Feelings column); the pictures can help students tell how a character feels.

5. **Wrap-Up**: Have students draw pictures of a character from a story. It can be Curious George or another character they have heard about. Each student should write one to three sentences, depending on the ability of your students at this point in the year. Each sentence should do one of the following: tell how the character looks, tell what the character did once, or tell how the character felt once.

Extend the Lesson

Read aloud another short book or fairy tale. Ask students to pay close attention to the characters as you read. Then play Who Am I? Say things such as, "I huffed and I puffed at the house. Who am I?" Ask three or more questions, using examples from different characters' looks, actions, and feelings. When students answer a question, follow up by asking, "How did you know that?" Perhaps there was a picture clue, or a student can retell part of the story.

Differentiation

For students who need extra support

- Draw picture clues on the three-column chart to help students read or remember the words *Looks, Actions,* and *Feelings.* For example, draw a magnifying glass next to Looks, a foot kicking a ball next to Actions, and a face with tears next to Feelings.

- For the wrap-up activity, ask students to draw and write about a specific character in a familiar fairy tale. With everyone working on the same character, you can provide hints or tips to the class or ask students to work in small groups.

For advanced students

- During the full-class activity, ask volunteers to write words in the chart for you.

- Ask students who finish the wrap-up activity quickly to use the remaining work time to choose a book from the class bookshelves and read about (or look at pictures of) a character that interests them.

Assessment

- Check students' work in the independent activity to make sure they write at least one valid word in each column of their charts.

- Make sure that students have drawn and written about a single character. Check for complete sentences, including end punctuation and capital letters. To assign a grade on a ten-point scale, give one point for each correct element: illustration, complete sentence, capital letter to begin sentence, and end punctuation for sentence (times three sentences).

Additional Resources

You can find different types of character work sheets and organizers online by using the search term *character work sheets* or *character organizer* to search Google images.

Sounds of the Letter *A*

> **Foundational Skills Mini-Lesson**

Common Core State Standards

1: Reading, Foundational Skills, Standard 3: Know and apply grade-level phonics and word analysis skills in decoding words. b. Decode regularly spelled one-syllable words.

c. Know final *e* and common vowel team conventions for representing long vowel sounds. g. Recognize and read grade-appropriate irregularly spelled words.

Planning and Preparation

- Gather supplies for students: pencils, scissors, and glue sticks.

- On paper that you can photocopy, prepare a three-column chart. Label the chart with a capital *A* and a lowercase *a*. Label column 1 Hat and draw a hat. Label column 2 Ball and draw a ball. Label column 3 Cake and draw a cake. Make copies for students and yourself.

- Use large type to list the following words on a sheet of paper that you can photocopy, keeping in mind that students will be cutting the page apart into one-word slips of paper. Make copies for students and yourself.

all	at	back	ball	day
fast	had	hand	hat	made
make	ran	sad	saw	was
way	what			

Agenda

1. Tell students that they are going to spend some time with words that are spelled with the letter *a*. Tell them *a* is a vowel.

2. Hold up the three-column chart, and explain that it has three parts. Read each word aloud, and point out the picture clue. Explain that the *a* sound is different in different words. Pronounce and explain the three *a* sounds represented on the chart. Have the students repeat the words aloud with you.

3. Hold up the paper with the word bank. Tell students the words are from the story they listened to, *Curious George's First Day of School*. Each of the words has the letter *a* in it.

4. Tell students that this is what they should do independently or in small groups:

   - Read a word in the word bank.
   - Decide what sound the *a* makes in the word.
   - Match the *a* sound to one of the *a* sounds in the chart.
   - Cut out the word, and glue it in the matching column of the chart.

     Note: You may wish to have students write the word in the chart instead of cutting and gluing.

5. Model the activity by going through steps a–c using one of the words in the word bank. Pass out the handouts and ask students to get started.

6. Taking the chart one column at a time, ask volunteers to read aloud words in each column of the chart. You may wish to fill in a master chart on the board during this activity.

Assessment

Check students' charts to see how consistently they decoded and sorted the words.   ■

Notes

After implementing the lesson, make notes on what worked and what you would change next time.

_____

_____

_____

_____

Character Activity Sheet

The character's name is _____ .

Tell about this character. Write words to describe the character in this chart.

Looks	Actions	Feelings
Examples: short, tall, hairy, thin, dirty	Examples: danced, ate cake, spilled paint	Examples: happy, curious, angry, surprised
Your words:	**Your words:**	**Your words:**

Step-by-Step

Describe Connections Between Steps in a Process

Lesson Plan 5

Grade Level: 2

Time Frame: Approximately one class period

Overview: In this lesson, students learn how ideas are connected in how-to texts, often with sequencing words such as *first*, *next*, and *after.* A text from the National Geographic website is used as a model, but you may want to use a how-to science text from your curriculum.

Common Core State Standards
- 2: Reading, Informational Text, Standard 3: Describe the connection between a series of historical events, scientific ideas or concepts, or steps in technical procedures in a text.
- 2: Writing, Standard 8: Recall information from experience or gather information from provided sources to answer a question.

Objectives
- Students will read the steps in a scientific procedure.
- Students will respond to sequencing words to answer questions about connections between steps in the procedure.
- Students will use sequencing words to tell how to complete a task.

Background Knowledge Required
No particular background knowledge is required for this lesson.

Materials Needed
- Copies of "Planting Seeds" (omitting the "Parent Tip" section): kidsblogs .nationalgeographic.com/littlekids/plant-seeds.html
- Copies of the handout: Steps in a Process Activity Sheet, p. 34

Agenda
1. **Introduction**: Ask students if anyone has ever grown a plant from a seed before. Engage students' interest by asking questions such as "What kind of plant did you grow?" "Did you grow it indoors or outdoors?" "What did you do to keep your plant alive?"

2. **Read Aloud**: Pass out copies of the article. Ask students to listen and follow along as you read it aloud. Be sure to read the numerals in the sequenced steps.

3. **Group Work**: Organize students into small groups. Pass out copies of the handout (one per student), and have group members work together to complete part 1 of the handout.

4. **Full-Class Discussion**: Go over students' answers in part 1 of the handout, using the discussion as an opportunity to point out the boldfaced sequencing words and to talk about the importance of completing tasks in order. Ask questions such as, "Look at the section called 'Here's How.' Why did the writer use numbers to list the sentences?" and "What would happen if you did step 4 first? What might go wrong?"

5. **Wrap-Up**: Ask students to complete part 2 of the handout independently.

Extend the Lesson

Explain that students can use sequencing words such as those in the word bank in the handout when they write informative texts and stories. Choose one of these genres to focus on, and explain how students might use sequencing words to tell about a volcanic eruption, for example, or write stories about events they imagine.

Differentiation

For students who need extra support

- Create text cards. Each card should contain one of the numbered steps from the "Here's How" section, but omit the sequencing numbers. Make multiple copies of the cards and distribute sets of cards to small groups.

- Have groups work to put the cards in order. As students look at their cards laid out in order, ask the questions in part 1 of the handout. Guide students through answering the questions, helping them "see" the answers in their cards.

For advanced students

- Ask volunteers to read their work in part 2 of the handout. Ask students to point out the sequencing words that they used.

Assessment

Evaluate students' work in part 2 of the handout. This rubric may be helpful for scoring.

Score	The student
4	▪ Tells how to do a task. ▪ Includes at least three steps. ▪ Puts the steps in a logical order. ▪ Uses at least two sequencing words.
3	▪ Tells how to do a task. ▪ Includes three steps, although a key step may be missing. ▪ Places one step out of the logical order. ▪ Uses one sequencing word.

2	• Tells how to do a task. • Includes two steps. • Might not use a sequencing word.
1	• Attempts to tell how to do a task but includes steps that are arranged illogically, that do not clearly connect, or that do not logically accomplish the task. • Does not use a sequencing word.
0	• Writes about a task but does not give steps for how to do the task.

Additional Resources

Cassandra Yorke, a Florida teacher, wrote a set of five mini-lessons, each ten to 15 minutes long, that work together to teach sequence. Four graphic organizers are included. The set is available in PDF at www.polk-fl.net/staff/teachers/reading/documents/DecemberFOCUSCalendarElem.pdf.

Spelling-Sound Correspondences

Common Core State Standards

2: Reading, Foundational Skills, Standard 3: Know and apply grade-level phonics and word analysis skills in decoding words. e. Identify words with inconsistent but common spelling-sound correspondences.

Planning and Preparation

No particular preparation is necessary for this mini-lesson.

Agenda

1. Tell students, "Sometimes, a letter works by itself to spell a sound. An example is the *a* in cat." Write *cat* on the board, and point to each letter as you pronounce the sound it makes; then blend the letters to say the word. Tell students that they are getting good at spelling lots of these kinds of words. Now, they are going to look at some letters that work as a team to spell one sound.

2. Write the word *soil* on the board. Say, "Let's take a look at this word. I will read it to you. *Soil*. Now read it with me: *soil*. Good! Now I'm going to read each letter in *soil*." Say each letter as you point to it. "Now I'm going to say each sound in *soil*." Say each sound as you point to the letter or letter pair that makes the sound. Underline *oi* as you pronounce the sound. Finally, say the entire word. "Do you see the *oi* here? These two letters work as a team. As a team, they make the *oi* sound in *soil*." Read each sound in the word again, and say the whole word again.

3. Ask students to take out writing paper. Have them write the word *soil*. Lead them in a choral reading of the letters (*s-o-i-l*) and then the sounds (*s-oi-l*). Finish by reading the complete word.

4. Write the word *noise* on the board. Repeat the process described in steps 2 and 3, above.

5. Write the word *join* on the board, and repeat the process, as above.

Assessment

Write an assortment of words on the board, including *foil, point, toil,* and *coin*. Include four other words that use an *o* or *i*, such as *oak, friend, look,* and *row*. Ask students to read the words silently. They should decide which words have a vowel team that makes the *oi* sound, as in *soil*. They should write those words on a fresh sheet of paper. Score students' work by awarding one point for each correct word (*foil, point, toil, coin*) and subtracting one point for each incorrect word. A top score is 4. ■

Notes

After implementing the lesson, make notes on what worked and what you would change next time.

_____

_____

_____

_____

Steps in a Process Activity Sheet

Part 1: Your teacher will read "Planting Seeds" to you. Listen and read along. Then answer these questions.

1. **Before** you plant seeds, what do you need to gather?

    - _____

    - _____

    - _____

2. You are ready to plant seeds. What is the **first** thing that you do?

    _____

3. What should you do right **after** you make two holes in the soil?

    _____

4. What should you do **before** you put the pot in a sunny window?

    _____

5. What is the **last** thing to do?

    _____

Part 2

Instructions: Think about something that you know how to do. Some ideas are listed in the box to the right. Tell how to do the task. Be sure to	**Ideas**

Instructions: Think about something that you know how to do. Some ideas are listed in the box to the right. Tell how to do the task. Be sure to

- Use at least three steps.

- Use words from the word bank to help show the order of the steps.

- Write on the lines below.

Word Bank

first	next	when
second	after	then
third	after that	last

Ideas

- brush your teeth

- get dressed for school

- make a sandwich

- set the table for dinner

How to _____

6. Tell how to do the task.

_____

_____

_____

_____

_____

_____

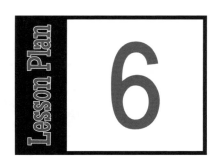

The Five W's and H

Answering Text-Based Questions

Grade Level: 2; can be adapted to other grades (see note in Overview)

Time Frame: Approximately three class periods

Overview: From kindergarten forward, the Common Core requires students to identify evidence in texts to answer questions about the texts. This is a shift from past pedagogical practices of asking for opinions, general observations, and personal responses that can be expressed without combing through a text's words, sentences, and paragraphs. This lesson focuses on questions that begin with *who, what, where, when, why,* and *how.* To get the info they need to answer such questions, students must dig into the words on the page. You can adapt this lesson to lower or higher grades by using just a few question types or by applying the questions to more complex texts. This lesson lends itself well to use with science, history, and technical texts.

Common Core State Standards
- 2: Reading, Informational Text, Standard 1: Ask and answer such questions as *who, what, where, when, why,* and *how* to demonstrate understanding of key details in a text.

- 2: Language, Standard 4: Determine or clarify the meaning of unknown and multiple-meaning words and phrases based on *grade 2 reading and content*, choosing flexibly from an array of strategies.

- 2: Language, Standard 6: Use words and phrases acquired through conversations, reading and being read to, and responding to texts.

- 2: Speaking and Listening, Standard 1: Participate in collaborative conversations with diverse partners about *grade 2 topics and texts* with peers and adults in small and larger groups.

- 2: Speaking and Listening, Standard 2: Recount or describe key ideas or details from a text read aloud or information presented orally or through other media.

Objectives
- Students will read a complex science text and answer questions that require a close analysis of what the words, sentences, and paragraphs mean.

- Students will work with peers to identify and explain key details in the text.

- Students will work with peers to use a dictionary and find the meaning of unfamiliar words.

Background Knowledge Required

Students should know that a "key" detail is an important detail in the passage, one that helps explain the main idea. How can readers know if a detail is key? If a key detail is left out, the text loses some of its meaning.

Materials Needed

- Copies of "Watch Out . . . Tornadoes Ahead!," available on NOAA's website: www.nws.noaa.gov/om/brochures/owlie-tornado.pdf

- Student dictionaries to pass out to small groups

Agenda

1. **Introduction**: On the board, write the words *Wild Weather*! and draw a tornado. Ask a volunteer to read the words, and ask volunteers to tell you what the picture shows and (briefly) what they know about tornadoes. Tell students that in this lesson, they will read and answer questions about tornadoes. Pass out copies of the informational text (omit the Tornado Quiz and the Answers page).

2. **Independent Reading**: Ask students to read the first page (the page labeled Tornadoes) of the handout independently. Tell students to be "active readers." This means that, as they read, they should underline unfamiliar words and put stars or check marks next to important ideas.

3. **Full-Class Reading**: Ask students to listen and follow along on their copies as you read Tornadoes aloud. Speak clearly and carefully, allowing students to hear the pronunciations of unfamiliar words and to hear the rhythm and cadence of the piece.

4. **Full-Class Discussion**: Lead students through an analysis of the text by asking a series of text-based questions. Each question should cause students to return to the text to reread a word, sentence, or paragraph in order to gather the facts or details needed to construct an answer. In grades K–3, text-based questions are designed to get students to identify and understand key details. In grades 4 and 5, students begin to draw conclusions from details in the text and point to details that support the conclusion. Here are some suggested questions:

   - How is a tornado like a regular cloud? How is it different? What details in the passage help you answer this question?
   - What is a tornado watch?
   - Why would the National Weather Service put out a tornado warning?
   - What are some signs that a tornado is coming?
   - How does a tornado flatten homes and throw cars around? What details in the passage help you answer this question?
   - If it's nighttime, how can you know that a tornado is coming? What detail does the passage give to help you remember how you can know a tornado is coming?

   Note: This is a good place to break the lesson into a second day.

5. **Full-Class Reading**: Read the remaining pages of the article aloud. Students should follow along on their own copies. Read slowly and clearly, and encourage students to take the time to underline unfamiliar words and place stars or check marks as you read.

6. **Dictionary Activity**: Ask volunteers to point out words in the passage that were unfamiliar. They should draw from the entire passage, not just today's reading. Make a list on the board. Organize students into small groups, and give each group a dictionary. Ask groups to look up the meanings of one or more words on the master list and write down definitions on their own paper. Finally, ask each group to share its results with the class. Next to each unfamiliar word in the passage, have students write keywords of the definition or draw picture clues to the word's meaning.

   Note: This is a good place to break the lesson into a third day.

7. **Passage Review**: As a full class, review the entire passage by going from page to page, asking students to point out ideas that they marked with stars or check marks.

8. **Group Work**: Pass out copies of the Tornado Quiz. In the "Fill in the blank" section, read aloud each word in the word bank, going slowly so that students can listen carefully to the pronunciation. Organize students into small groups. Have group members work together to complete the "Fill in the blank" items.

9. **Wrap-Up**: Have groups share their answers to the Tornado Quiz. As you discuss each answer, remind students that these keywords connect to key ideas in the passage. Ask them which words in the word bank they underlined in the passage as unfamiliar. Which words did they know already? Remind students that keywords in a passage are not always new and strange sounding. Sometimes, keywords are familiar.

Extend the Lesson

- Don't worry if you don't have time to cover all the above questions during class time. You can use the additional questions to extend the lesson to another day, to use in a homework assignment, or to use as a writing assignment.

- Tell students that stories can teach information too. Ask students to use the information they learned in "Watch Out . . . Tornadoes Ahead!" to write a story about a child and a tornado. Have them use some of the words in the Tornado Quiz word bank in their story. To bring in the connection between illustrations and texts (RL.2.7 and RI.2.7), you can have students draw or find pictures to go with their stories.

Differentiation

For students who need extra support

- Spend more time helping students work out the meanings of unfamiliar words using various strategies, such as context clues, peer input, and reference sources.

- For homework, ask students to write in complete sentences to answer one of the text-based questions discussed in class. This reinforces the message that close textual readings require multiple readings of the same passage. Readers' understanding of the text deepens over time.

For advanced students

- Ask volunteers to read paragraphs of the passage aloud during the full-class reading.

- For homework, ask students to write in complete sentences to answer a text-based question that was not discussed in class. As with struggling students, the advanced students will receive the message that multiple readings are beneficial, and they will be challenged to find new connections and meaning in the text.

Assessment

- Check students' work on the Tornado Quiz to see that they used the keywords correctly.

- Use the following rubric to evaluate students' written or oral responses to a text-based question.

Score 4.0	The student
	▪ Refers to or uses multiple words, phrases, or sentences in the text to answer the question.
	▪ Logically links the evidence (in first bullet) to the text-based question.
	▪ Expresses a clear answer to the question using the evidence and logic in the previous bullets.
	No major errors or omissions in the score 4.0 content.
Score 3.5	The student demonstrates success at the 3.0 level plus partial success at the 4.0 level.
Score 3.0	The student
	▪ Refers to at least one word, phrase, or sentence in the text in the response.
	▪ Logically links the evidence (in first bullet) to the text-based question.
	▪ Attempts to express an answer to the question.
	No major errors or omissions in the score 3.0 content.
Score 2.5	The student demonstrates success at the 2.0 level plus partial success at the 3.0 level.
Score 2.0	The student
	▪ Refers vaguely to ideas in the text to answer the question.
	▪ Links (however loosely) the evidence (in first bullet) to the text-based question.
	No major errors or omissions in the score 2.0 content.
Score 1.5	The student demonstrates partial success at the 2.0 level; responses may identify evidence in the text but fail to use it to answer the question or may answer the question without using specific evidence from the text.
Score 1.0	With help, the student achieves partial success at score 2.0 and 3.0 contents; responses are simplistic and limited.
Score 0.5	With help, the student achieves partial success at score 2.0 content but not score 3.0 content.
Score 0.0	Even with help, the student has no success.

Additional Resources

Get ideas for designing your own *Who, What, Where, When, Why, How* work sheet by typing in these question words plus *work sheet* in a browser's image search.

Foundational Skills
Mini-Lesson

Irregularly Spelled Words

Common Core State Standards

2: Reading, Foundational Skills, Standard 3: Know and apply grade-level phonics and word analysis skills in decoding words. f. Recognize and read grade-appropriate irregularly spelled words.

Planning and Preparation

On a sheet of paper, create word cards using the following words. Make a copy for each student plus yourself. Cut the cards apart. **Note**: These words were drawn from "Watch Out . . . Tornadoes Ahead!," but you can use words that you select.

ahead	cloud
listen	roar

On a sheet of paper, create bookmark-shaped lists for each word, modeled after the following one. Make a copy for each student plus yourself. Cut the lists apart.

Name: _____

1. roar
2. r __ ar
3. r __ __ r
4. r __ __ __
5. __ __ __ __
6. _____

Agenda

1. Tell students that in some words, some letters do not follow regular spelling patterns. They are called irregularly spelled words. Tell students that they are going to read and write some irregularly spelled words.

2. On the *roar* word card, point to the word as you read it aloud. Explain that in *roar*, some of the letters do not make their usual sounds. Point to each letter as you spell *roar*; then read the word aloud again. Repeat the process, this time telling students that you will trace each letter with your finger as you say its name. Read the word aloud again.

3. Pass out *roar* word cards. Take students through the process with you. First, ask them to point to each letter as everyone reads each letter aloud. Then read the word aloud as a class. Then students should trace each letter with a pencil as they read each letter aloud. Then read the word aloud as a class.

4. Pass out the bookmark-shaped activity sheet for *roar.* Tell students that they will learn to spell *roar.*

   - Step 1: As a class, read the word aloud.
   - Step 2: Ask a volunteer to identify the missing letter. Ask everyone to write it in the blank. As a class, spell and then read the word aloud.
   - Steps 3–5: Repeat the process.
   - Step 6: Have students write the word *roar* without the letter-cue blanks and then read the word aloud.

5. Repeat the exercise in agenda item 4 for each word card.

Assessment

Write the words from this mini-lesson on the board. Calling on each student in turn, point to a word and ask the student to spell and say the word. Make notes of words that all students find challenging. Also make notes of students who need additional work with this set of words. ■

Notes

After implementing the lesson, make notes on what worked and what you would change next time.

_____

_____

_____

_____

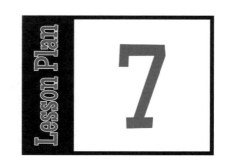

More Than One Way to Tell a Story

Distinguish Among Stories, Dramas, and Poems

Lesson Plan 7

Grade Level: 3

Time Frame: Approximately three to four class periods

Overview: The Common Core introduces drama to students for the first times in grade 3. The focus at this level is to teach students to distinguish among genres (stories, dramas, poems) and to use appropriate academic vocabulary to speak or write about works in each genre. In grades 4 and 5, students build on this knowledge by learning to examine structural elements of genres. This lesson helps students see the big picture: How are stories, dramas, and poems different from one another?

Common Core State Standards

- 3: Reading, Literature, Standard 5: Refer to parts of stories, dramas, and poems when writing or speaking about a text, using terms such as *chapter, scene,* and *stanza*; describe how each successive part builds on earlier sections.

- 3: Speaking and Listening, Standard 1: Engage effectively in a range of collaborative discussions . . . with diverse partners on *grade 3 topics and texts,* building on others' ideas and expressing their own clearly.

- 3: Speaking and Listening, Standard 4: Report on a topic or text, tell a story, or recount an experience with appropriate facts and relevant descriptive details, speaking clearly at an understandable pace.

- 3: Language, Standard 6: Acquire and use accurately grade-appropriate conversational, general academic, and domain-specific words and phrases.

Objectives

- Students will examine an excerpt from a story, using academic vocabulary to describe elements of a story (*chapter, paragraph,* etc.).

- Students will examine a play, using academic vocabulary to describe elements of drama (*actor, scene,* etc.).

- Students will examine a poem, using academic vocabulary to describe elements of poetry (*line, stanza,* etc.).

- Students will participate in a reader's theater, reading lines of a play aloud.

- Students will work with peers to prepare and deliver a shared oral report that identifies elements of stories, plays, and poems.

Background Knowledge Required

Students should know how to recognize stories and poems as separate genres, or types, of literature.

Materials Needed

- A copy of *Herbie Jones and the Class Gift*, by Suzy Kline

- Photocopies of the first page of chapter 1 in *Herbie Jones and the Class Gift*, for students

- A copy of *The Herbie Jones Reader's Theater: Funny Scenes to Read Aloud*, by Suzy Kline

- Photocopies of "The Class Gift," pages 101–108, in *The Herbie Jones Reader's Theater*

- Copies of the handout: Types of Literature Activity Sheet, p. 47

Agenda

1. **Introduction**: Tell students that today you would like to introduce them to a boy their age. His name is Herbie Jones. He is not a real-life boy, however. Herbie Jones lives in books and plays written by Suzy Kline. To tell a little about Herbie Jones, refer to the paragraph-long character sketch on page 7 of the *Reader's Theater*.

2. **Read Aloud**: Read aloud chapter 1 of *Herbie Jones and the Class Gift*. This takes eight to ten minutes; if this is too much time, you might choose to read the first three to four pages instead. The important thing is that students get an idea of what the story is about.

3. **Full-Class Discussion**: Pass out copies of page 1 of the chapter you read aloud. Point out and explain key elements of a story (see the handout for key elements). As you talk, create a list on the board labeled Stories, listing the key elements.

4. **Group Work**: Organize students into small groups, and pass out copies of the handout. Have students work together to complete the Stories section of the handout.

   Note: You can break the lesson here, continuing on another day.

5. **Introduce the Drama**: Pass out copies of "The Class Gift" from the *Reader's Theater*, pages 101–108. Point out and explain key elements of a drama (play). See the handout for key elements. As you talk, create a list of key elements on the board, labeled Dramas.

6. **Dramatic Reading**: Tell students that plays are meant to be performed in front of an audience. They can perform this play right here in the classroom. Assign speaking roles to students. You can assign more than one student to a character, with the second student taking over partway through the reading. If you are short on time, ask each student to read a character's lines until each student has read once.

7. **Group Work**: Organize students into small groups. Have students work together to complete the Dramas (Plays) section of the handout.

   Note: You can break the lesson here, continuing on another day.

8. **Introduce the Poem**: Direct students' attention to pages 106–107 of the play. Ask a volunteer to point out the poem. Explain that poems are another type of literature. Explain key elements of poems (see the handout for key terms). List the keywords you discuss, and label it Poems.

9. **Group Work**: Organize students into small groups. Have students work together to complete the Poems section of the handout.

10. **Wrap-Up**: Ask volunteers to share their responses on the handout.

Extend the Lesson

Have students create genre-based reader's logs in their notebooks, labeling pages Stories, Dramas, and Poems. Ask students to keep logs during the school year, writing down the names of each story, drama, and poem that they read (or see, in the case of dramas). Follow up on this assignment periodically throughout the year, using discussion, writing, or speaking assignments, to affirm students' reading and to build academic vocabulary into their long-term memories.

Differentiation

For students who need extra support

- Use just a short segment of the story and drama to teach the concepts, focusing on explaining keywords and their pronunciations and examining the formats of the genres. If students are curious about what happens in the rest of the chapter or drama, read the entire pieces another day.

For advanced students

- During the reader's theater, assign advanced students the roles of Herbie, Annabelle, and Raymond because these have longer speaking parts. When reviewing the poem, ask a volunteer to read the poem aloud.

Assessment

Have students work in groups of three to create shared oral reports that explain three types of literature: stories, dramas, and poems. Each group member should prepare and deliver one part of the group's report. In their reports, students should use key academic vocabulary. Remind students to use the notes they wrote on their handouts to prepare for their oral report. You can assign grades based on points that students earn, with 4 being a top score.

Points to Earn	Task
1	Works with peers to organize responsibilities for the oral report.
1	Prepares one section of the oral report, giving accurate information.
1	Presents one section of the oral report, giving accurate information.
1	Uses one or more academic vocabulary words accurately.
Top Score: 4	

Additional Resources

- ReadWriteThink's lesson plan "What Makes Poetry? Exploring Line Breaks" (grades 3–5) is available online at www.readwritethink.org/classroom-resources/lesson-plans/what-makes-poetry-exploring-88.html.

- A very short printable play, "Mary Chestnut and her Diary," is available on the Scholastic website: printables.scholastic.com/content/collateral_resources/pdf/00/SPB00_185.pdf.

- A four-act play, "The Boston Massacre," is available on the Scholastic website: printables.scholastic.com/content/collateral_resources/pdf/55/0590033255_e001.pdf. Pages at the end of the play provide historical background, related readings, and activities.

Introduction to Syllables

> **Foundational Skills Mini-Lesson**

Common Core State Standards

3: Reading, Foundational Skills, Standard 3: Know and apply grade-level phonics and word analysis skills in decoding words. c. Decode multisyllable words.

Planning and Preparation

Gather one small mirror per student. If this isn't feasible, ask students to work in pairs in agenda item 3; they can act as each other's mirror.

Agenda

1. Write the word *syllable* on the board, and say it aloud. Tell the class that a syllable is one sound chunk in a word. Demonstrate by clapping or tapping out each syllable in *syllable* as you say the word again. Say the word a third time, this time drawing slash marks to divide the syllables (*syl/la/ble*). Ask, "How many syllables are in this word? Yes! There are three sound chunks in the word *syllable*."

2. Explain that students can count syllables in a word by counting how many times they move their jaws when they say the word. (If necessary, review what a jaw is.) Demonstrate by repeating *syllable* with exaggerated jaw movements, saying, "Did you see that? I moved my jaw three times to say that word. My jaw had to help my mouth make each sound chunk." Demonstrate saying *syllable* again.

3. Pass out small mirrors to students. Now they get to watch their own jaws move as they say words. Write the first sentence from *Herbie Jones and the Class Gift* on the board: "Herbie Jones hated indoor recess." Guide students to say each word aloud while watching their jaws move. Count the syllables in each word. Draw slash marks to separate syllables, and write the number of syllables below each word.

4. Repeat the exercise with additional sentences from the passage or with words or sentences you choose. The *Herbie Jones* passage has mainly one- and two-syllable

words, so you may want to use a social studies or science text next. Consider count-ing the syllables in students' names too.

5. If you think students are ready to add a level of complexity to the mini-lesson, exam-ine a few words that have common prefixes and suffixes. Help students see that a prefix or suffix forms its own syllable.

Assessment

Prepare a list of words, either a selection of words used in the mini-lesson or new ones you choose, and make copies for students. Ask students to count the syllables in each word and to write down the number. If students are struggling, have them work in pairs to complete the assignment. Check their work to see if they grasp the concept of a syllable. ■

Notes

After implementing the lesson, make notes on what worked and what you would change next time.

_____

_____

_____

_____

Name: _____   Date: _____

Types of Literature Activity Sheet

Read each section of the chart. Write facts that you know about each word in the list.

Stories	Dramas (Plays)
How can you tell if something is a story? Look for these things:	How can you tell if something is a drama? Look for these things:
▪ sentences	▪ cast of characters
▪ paragraphs	▪ settings
▪ chapter numbers	▪ scenes
▪ chapter titles	▪ characters' names with lines to speak
Remember that short stories don't have chapters, but books do.	▪ stage directions

Poems

How can you tell if something is a poem? Look for these things:

- one or more stanzas

- lines

- rhymes

Note: Some poems use words that rhyme, and other poems do not use rhyme.

Who Is Telling This Story?

Point of View in Stories

Grade Level: 3

Time Frame: Approximately two class periods

Overview: Beginning in grade 1, students learn to identify who is telling a story. As they progress from grade to grade, their analyses of a narrator extend to include characters' points of view within a story, narrative point of view (first person vs. third person), and the connection between narrative point of view and the presentation of events. This lesson teaches the basics of identifying the point of view of a character, narrator, or reader. Though it is designed for grade 3, it is useful for reviewing the concepts at most elementary grade levels.

Common Core State Standards

- 3: Reading, Literature, Standard 6: Distinguish their own point of view from that of the narrator or those of the characters.

- 3: Writing, Standard 3: Write narratives to develop real or imagined experiences or events using effective technique, descriptive details, and clear event sequences.

- 3: Writing, Standard 10: Write routinely over extended time frames . . . and shorter time frames . . . for a range of discipline-specific tasks, purposes, and audiences.

- 3: Language, Standard 6: Acquire and accurately use grade-appropriate conversational, general academic, and domain-specific words and phrases.

Objectives

- Students will identify who is telling a story.

- Students will answer questions to distinguish among different characters' points of view and their own points of view on events of a story.

- Students will write narrative paragraphs about a sequence of events they witness.

- Students will learn the terms *narrator* and *point of view*.

Background Knowledge Required

Students should be familiar with the terms *character* and *point of view* from their work in grade 2.

Materials Needed

- Copies of a book or story that students are reading for class

- Copies of the handout: Point of View Activity Sheet, p. 54

Agenda

1. **Introduction**: Write *point of view* on the board, and briefly explain the term by saying something such as "Point of view is how a certain person sees the events of a story. This person could be the person who is telling the story. It could be a character in the story. It could be you, the readers. Each character and person has his or her own point of view about what happens."

2. **Demonstration**: To illustrate point of view, tell students that you want them to watch closely what you do and then write paragraphs that tell what they saw.

   - Enact a simple skit of one or two minutes. For example, leave the classroom, and then reenter holding a mysterious box. Walk into the room, and stand so that only some students can see the box. Open the box, and examine what's inside (something that makes a sound, such as a jingle bell or aluminum foil, works well). Put the object back in the box, and exit the room.

   - Come back into the room, and ask each student to write one paragraph telling what he or she saw. As students work on their paragraphs, write a brief paragraph describing the event from your point of view.

   - Ask volunteers from different parts of the room to read their paragraphs. Ask, "What did you see from your point of view?" Compare and contrast writers' points of view. "From Carlos's point of view, the item in the box was a big mystery that was never solved. But from Olivia's point of view, the item in the box was a mystery that got solved. From Nick's point of view, the item in the box was a funny surprise. But from Maddy's point of view, the item was a disappointment after all that suspense." Point out how people's understanding of what happens is different depending on what details they can see and hear. Read your own paragraph, contrasting details of your viewpoint to the details of observers' points of view.

   - Tell students that stories are like life when it comes to point of view. Different characters and the narrator (the person who tells the story) see events from their own points of view.

   Note: You can break the lesson here and continue on another day.

3. **Full-Class Activity**: Ask students to take out a story they have been reading for class. Examine the story with them, asking questions to help them think about the narrator's and different characters' points of view of events in the story. Also ask questions to help students realize that they, as readers, have yet another point of view. Some of the following text-based questions may be useful:

   - Who is telling the story? How do you know? The person who tells the story is called the *narrator*.

   - Is the narrator a character in the story or a voice from outside telling the story? How can you tell?

- What does _____ (name a character) know that one or more other characters don't know?
- Does the narrator know what one or more characters are thinking? Or feeling? What sentence or paragraph helps you answer this question?
- Do you think this part is funny (or sad, confusing, suspenseful, etc.)? Why? Do you think _____ (name a character) would agree with you, or does he/she have a different point of view? Why is that? (For example, think of "Split Pea Soup," in which George is tired of eating Martha's soup and hides his serving of soup in his shoe. This action is funny to the reader but not to George. In suspenseful stories, an event may seem frightening or mysterious from both the main character's and the reader's points of view, while the villain's point of view is entirely different.)

4. **Wrap-Up**: Have students complete the handout for homework or an in-class activity. As a full class, review students' responses, using the discussion as an opportunity to review the key terms *narrator* and *point of view*.

Differentiation

For students who need extra support

- Group students in pairs or small groups to complete the handout, or complete the handout together as a class.

For advanced students

- During the wrap-up, ask volunteers to provide definitions and examples for the key terms, writing their definitions on the board. Ask volunteers to tell the class the names of stories they have read and who the narrators of the stories are.

Assessment

- Collect students' paragraphs from the demonstration activity. For students who need extra support, circle key details that they noticed from their point of view and write a note of confirmation: "These are good examples of what you saw from your point of view." For advanced students, circle a few instances of first-person, second-person, or third-person pronouns and write a comment: "You did a great job of using the pronoun *I* to tell about events from your point of view" or "Great job of writing about your point of view as if you were speaking directly to me, the reader" or "Great job of writing about what you saw as if you were a storyteller watching the action."

- Check students' work on the handout, looking not just for correct answers but also for how well students used details or examples from the text to answer questions 2, 3, and 5. If students have difficulty selecting relevant details for these questions, create a second handout using a different fable but similar questions. Complete the handout as a class and demonstrate how to look for relevant details to help answer a question.

Additional Resources

- A selection of Aesop's fables is available on Professor Copper Giloth's page on the University of Massachusetts website: www.umass.edu/aesop/.

Prefixes and Suffixes

Common Core State Standards

3: Reading, Foundational Skills, Standard 3: Know and apply grade-level phonics and word analysis skills in decoding words. a. Identify and know the meaning of the most common prefixes and derivational suffixes. b. Decode words with common Latin suffixes. c. Decode multisyllable words.

Planning and Preparation

Prepare a copy of the following chart to photocopy for the class. The prefixes and suffixes in the chart are used in the activity that follows. If you wish, add additional prefixes and suffixes to the chart, and extend the activity to include them. You can have a little fun by using the theme of mystery to title the page and choose icons for the borders. For example: "Here is the <u>code</u> you need to <u>decode</u> words when they are a mystery to you!"

	Prefix or Suffix	Meaning	Examples
Prefixes (beginning word parts)	1. de-	1. not, remove	1. defrost, deplane
	2. mis-	2. bad, wrong	2. mislead, misspell
	3. re-	3. again	3. reheat, remove
	4. un-	4. not	4. untie, undress
Suffixes (ending word parts)	1. -dom	1. used to form a noun	1. freedom, fiefdom
	2. -ly	2. in a certain way	2. quickly, cowardly
	3. -ous	3. connected to	3. joyous, humorous
	4. -y	4. condition	4. curly, grouchy

Write a list of questions about "The Ant and the Grasshopper" that will require students to identify or use prefixes and suffixes in their answers. Make copies for students. Here are some suggested questions:

- Read the last paragraph of the story. Which word uses the suffix *-ly*?

- Read the third paragraph. Which word uses the prefix *re-*?

- The word *envious* is made up of *envy* plus the suffix *-ous*. What do you think Grasshopper was envious of?

- The word *mistake* is made up of the word *take* plus the prefix *mis-*. What was Grasshopper's mistake?

- Grasshopper was hungry in the winter. How can you use the suffix *-y* and the word *winter* to make an adjective? Write the new word here: _____

Agenda

1. Tell students that a prefix is a word part added to the beginning of a word to make a new word. Write the word *unpack* on the board. Ask a volunteer to come up and circle the prefix in the word.

2. Tell students that another kind of word part is a suffix. People add suffixes to the ends of words to make new words. Write the word *kingdom* on the board. Ask a volunteer to come up and circle the suffix in the word.

3. Pass out copies of the prefix and suffix chart. Explain that words are like a code. Readers have to know what each part of a word means to figure out the word's meaning. Readers who know the meanings of prefixes and suffixes can decode many more words. Write the word *decode* on the board. Ask a volunteer to tell you whether the word has a prefix or a suffix. Ask another volunteer to come up and circle the prefix.

4. Pass out the questions you prepared and ask students to write an answer to each question.

Assessment

Check students' written responses to the questions. If students are struggling, go over the questions as a class and ask volunteers to share their answers.   ■

Notes

After implementing the lesson, make notes on what worked and what you would change next time.

_____

_____

_____

_____

Point of View Activity Sheet

Read the story. Then answer the questions.

The Ant and the Grasshopper
based on the tale by Aesop

In a field one summer's day, Grasshopper was hopping about. He chirped and sang to his heart's content. What a happy Grasshopper he was! Just then, Ant passed by, bearing an ear of corn that he was taking to the nest.

"Why not come and chat with me," said the Grasshopper. "It would be much more fun than working so hard!"

Ant stopped to rearrange his load. "I am helping to store up food for the winter," said Ant. "I suggest that you do the same."

"Why bother about winter?" asked Grasshopper. "We have plenty of food at present." But Ant went on his way and continued his work.

When winter came, Grasshopper found himself dying of hunger. Sadly, he watched the ants eating corn and grain from the stores they had collected in the summer. What an unhappy Grasshopper he was. Then Grasshopper thought, *"It is best to prepare for the days of necessity."*

1. Who is telling the story? Is it Ant, Grasshopper, or someone who is not in the story?

   _____

2. Look at your answer to question 1. How do you know that the narrator is (or is not) a character in the story?

   _____

   _____

3. At the beginning of the story, what important lesson does Ant know that Grasshopper doesn't know?

   _____

   _____

4. Whose thoughts does the narrator tell at the end of the story?

   _____

5. Think about the hard work that Ant did.

   - How can you tell that Ant thinks the hard work is worth it? Use a detail from the story to answer the question.

     _____

     _____

   - How can you tell that Grasshopper thinks the hard work is not worth it? Use a detail from the story to answer the question.

     _____

     _____

Sometimes Words Aren't Enough

Interpret Visual Elements

Grade Level: 4; can be adapted to other grades (see note in Overview)

Time Frame: Approximately one or two class periods

Overview: This lesson teaches students to identify visual elements in an informational text and explain how a graphic helps them understand ideas in the text. The examples are drawn from grade 4, but you can easily adapt the lesson to another grade level (K–5) by selecting texts with visual elements listed in the desired grade's Informational Text Standard 7.

Common Core State Standards

- 4: Reading, Informational Text, Standard 7: Interpret information presented visually, orally, or quantitatively (e.g., in charts, graphs, diagrams, time lines, animations, or interactive elements on webpages) and explain how the information contributes to an understanding of the text in which it appears.

- 4: Speaking and Listening, Standard 1: Engage effectively in a range of collaborative discussions . . . with diverse partners on *grade 4 topics and texts*, building on others' ideas and expressing their own clearly.

- 4: Language, Standard 6: Acquire and use grade-appropriate general academic and domain-specific words and phrases, including those . . . that are basic to a particular topic.

Objectives

- Students will identify charts, graphs, diagrams, and/or time lines in an informational text.

- Students will explain how visual elements contribute to their understanding of ideas in the text.

- Students will work collaboratively in small groups to complete tasks and will contribute ideas to full-class discussions.

Background Knowledge Required

Students should be familiar with identifying the main idea or topic of a text.

Materials Needed

- A dozen or so informational books that use such visual elements as charts, graphs, diagrams, and time lines. You may want to choose books that relate to topics the students are studying in social studies, science, and math. In each book, use a sticky note to mark a page with a visual element that you would like students to examine.

- Copies of the handout: Visual Elements Activity Sheet, p. 61

Agenda

1. **Introduction**: Set up a display of the informational books. Tell students that these books are on different topics but have something in common. They give information about a topic. Hold up one of the books, and flip through pages so students can see the mix of text and diagrams or other visual elements. Explain that informational texts sometimes use visual elements to help readers understand the ideas and information. As a memory cue, draw a pair of eyes on the board and write the term *visual elements* next to the drawing. Then write the definition "things other than words in a book or an article." Tell students that today, they will work with partners (or in small groups) to identify and explain the connection between a visual element and the information in one of these books.

2. **Pairs (or Small Group) Activity**: Depending on the number of books you have, organize students into pairs or small groups. Each group should have one book from the display. Have each group complete questions 1–4 on the handout.

3. **Academic Vocabulary**: Ask the groups to stop their work for a few minutes. Briefly identify and explain the types of visual elements that you have marked in the books. List the terms on the board. As you teach each term, ask students to say the term aloud with you. Finally, ask students to work again with their partners or groups to answer question 5 on the handout.

   Note: You can break the lesson here and continue with the wrap-up and the lesson extension on another day.

4. **Wrap-Up**: Have each pair or small group share its book and handout with the full class. If you are short on time, ask just one group per type of visual element to share. To review the ideas another day, you can have the other groups share.

Extend the Lesson

- Have students use a dictionary, an encyclopedia, or a glossary that you find or create to look up each type of visual element. They can do this in conjunction with the academic vocabulary discussion and/or wrap-up.

- Have students create posters to hang in the classroom. Each poster should name a visual element, tell why it is useful, and include a sketch or drawing of an example of that kind of visual element.

- Use the lesson plan two or more times, each time focusing on just one type of visual element.

Differentiation

For students who need extra support

▪ In advance of the lesson, prepare posters like those described in the lesson extension activity. Review these posters during the academic vocabulary part of the lesson and, if needed, during the wrap-up. As you teach lessons in other subjects that use these visual elements, review relevant posters again.

For advanced students

▪ Ask advanced students to speak for their groups in the wrap-up activity.

Assessment

▪ Monitor students' work during the pairs or small group activity. Pay attention to their sketches of the visual element in question 3. Remind students to include key details of the element, such as labels or multiple images in a sequence.

▪ Award points for each correct answer to a question on the handout, based on the complexity of the question. For example: question 1 = 1 point; question 2 = 2 points; question 3 = 2 points; question 4 = 3 points; question 5 = 2 points (for a total of 10 points).

Additional Resources

▪ Kid-friendly definitions of different types of visual elements are available in the Merriam-Webster Word Central kids' dictionary: www.wordcentral.com.

▪ Suggested topics for the model informational texts include insects, frogs (life cycle), butterflies (life cycle), plants, constellations, the human body, volcanoes, and dinosaurs. An example text is *Incredible Insects* (in the Ranger Rick NatureScope series), by the National Wildlife Federation. This book has a line graph, a bar graph, and many diagrams.

Word Analysis Skills

> Foundational Skills
> Mini-Lesson

Common Core State Standards

▪ 4: Reading, Foundational Skills, Standard 3: Know and apply grade-level phonics and word analysis skills in decoding words. a. Use combined knowledge of all letter-sound correspondences, syllabification patterns, and morphology (e.g., roots and affixes) to accurately read unfamiliar multisyllabic words in context and out of context.

▪ 4: Reading, Foundational Skills, Standard 4: Read with sufficient accuracy and fluency to support comprehension. c. Use context to confirm or self-correct word recognition and understanding, rereading as necessary.

Planning and Preparation

Choose a short passage at your students' reading level that also contains a few challenging words. Make sure the passage has a related visual element, such as a diagram, or find one to use (see the third bulleted item under 3 in the agenda below). Make copies of the passage and visual element to pass out. Here is a suggested passage. A useful visual element would be a diagram, photograph, or sketch of a honeycomb.

1. First the worker bees collect nectar from flowers, sucking it up with their tongues and storing it in their honey stomachs, called *crops.*

2. Once their stomachs are full, the worker bees go back to the hive and transfer the nectar to other worker bees. (They do this by regurgitating the nectar into the mouths of the hive bees.) The hive bees then store the nectar in cells in the comb.

> —from "A Taste of Honey" in *Incredible Insects* (National Wildlife Federation, Chelsea House Publishers, 1997, p. 47).

Agenda

1. Read the passage aloud, proceeding slowly rather than quickly and pronouncing words clearly. Ask students to follow along on their copies.
2. Ask students to read the passage independently. Have them circle any unfamiliar words.
3. Tell students that all readers come across unfamiliar words, whether they are beginning or advanced readers. Readers can figure out unfamiliar words by using a few tricks of the trade.

   - **Look at the word parts**. Do you recognize a prefix? A suffix? Use this clue to make a guess about the word's meaning. Does your guess make sense in the passage? If yes, then your guess is probably right!

     Ask a volunteer to point out a word that has a prefix or suffix. Think aloud to figure out the word's meaning: "This word is *transfer*. I know that *trans* means "across," as in the words *transaction* and *transport*. Based on this clue, I think that *transfer* means 'to move across.' Yes, this makes sense in the sentence."
   - **Use context clues**. *Context* is the words or sentences around an unfamiliar word. Context can give readers a clue to the word's meaning. Use the clue to make a guess about the word's meaning. Does your guess make sense in the passage? If yes, then your guess is probably right!

     Ask a volunteer to point out an unfamiliar word, or point one out yourself. Think aloud to figure out the meaning: "This word is *crops*. What does *crops* have to do with bees? Oh, this sentence says that bees' honey stomachs are called crops. Here's another example: What does *regurgitating* mean? The bees do this into the mouths of other bees. It's an action. It gets the honey from their stomachs into the other bees' mouths. This sounds like throwing up into the other bee's mouth! Yes, that makes sense in this paragraph."
   - **Use pictures, diagrams, or other visual elements** to figure out the word's meaning. For example, you may not remember what a thorax is. A diagram that

labels the middle section of an insect's body as a *thorax* can help you figure out the word's meaning.

Ask a volunteer to point out a word that the visual element in the passage helps make clear. Think aloud to model the thought process: "The nectar is stored in *cells* in the comb. Based on the picture, I'm sure that *comb* means *honeycomb*. But what are *cells*? Oh, they are probably these little roundish sections in the honeycomb."

Assessment

Select another short passage and accompanying visual element in a textbook, or pass out copies (if students are not allowed to write in the textbook). Read the passage aloud. Then ask students to read the passage independently, marking unfamiliar words. On a separate sheet of paper, they should list three unfamiliar words from the passage. Next to each word, they should list two things: a clue to the word's meaning and the word's meaning. Review students' work for accuracy. If they are struggling, repeat the mini-lesson, using the passage you used in the assessment.   ■

Notes

After implementing the lesson, make notes on what worked and what you would change next time.

_____

_____

_____

_____

Visual Elements Activity Sheet

Use the words and the visual elements in a book or an article to answer these questions.

1. What is the book's title?

_____

2. Turn to the page that your teacher marked with a sticky note.

- What is this page or section of the book mostly about? This is the main idea.

_____

- What are some words or phrases from the book that help you identify the main idea?

_____

_____

3. Find a visual element that helps explain part of the text. In the box, draw or sketch the visual element.

4. How does the visual element help explain part of the text? For example, does it help you create a mental image of different amounts? Does it show you the parts of an insect? Does it organize information into categories? Does it arrange dates and information in order? Use details or examples from the text in your answer.

_____

_____

_____

_____

5. Look at the visual element that you described in questions 3 and 4.

- Name the type of visual element.

_____

- What parts of the visual element helped you identify it?

_____

_____

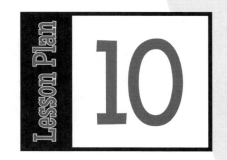

A Special Message from the Author

Lesson Plan 10

Determine Topics and Theme in a Story

Grade Levels: 4–5

Time Frame: Approximately two class periods

Overview: Beginning in grade 2, students are asked to determine a theme—a central message, lesson, or moral—in stories. This lesson reviews this crucial skill, emphasizing the use of details and topics in the text to determine theme. In the following lesson, "The Same—but Not Really!," students will build on these skills by comparing and contrasting themes in different stories. The picture storybooks by Chris Van Allsburg were chosen for these two lessons because of the complexity of the story concepts and ideas that unfold throughout the plots. You can choose alternate texts.

Common Core State Standards
- 4: Reading, Literature, Standard 1: Refer to details and examples in a text when explaining what the text says explicitly and when drawing inferences from the text.

- 4: Reading, Literature, Standard 2: Determine a theme of a story, drama, or poem from details in the text; summarize the text.

- 5: Reading, Literature, Standard 2: Determine a theme of a story, drama, or poem from details in the text, including how characters in a story or drama respond to challenges or how the speaker in a poem reflects upon a topic; summarize the text.

Objectives
- Students will identify topics in an adventure story.

- Students will determine themes in an adventure story, using details and examples from the story to support and explain a theme.

Background Knowledge Required
Students should be familiar with the concept of central lesson, message, or moral from previous grades.

Materials Needed
- Copy of *Just a Dream*, by Chris Van Allsburg, to read aloud

- Large poster boards or chart paper, enough to give one to each of five to seven small groups

- A marker for each small group

Agenda

1. **Introduction**: Using the central topic of dreams, create a model idea map on the board. Show students how they can start with an idea, link topics to it, and link ideas and examples to the topics. Ask volunteers to help you construct the idea web.

2. **Small Groups**: Organize students into small groups, and give each group a poster board and marker. Ask students to listen as you read a few pages from *Just a Dream*.

3. **Read and Think**
    *   Read the title and author's name. Read the first nine pages, letting students see the pictures. This takes three to five minutes. Stop reading after the scene with the bulldozer in the garbage dump.
    *   Ask each group to use its poster board to create an idea map with the words *Topics in Just a Dream* in the center circle. Students should identify two topics in the story so far and write them on spokes that connect to the center. Examples may include recycling, dreaming, garbage, and the future. Students should connect one or more details from the story to each topic.

4. **Read and Think**: Repeat the process from the read and think activity above, this time reading the next 16 pages, through the scene with the fishermen. This takes four to six minutes. Ask groups to add topics and supporting details to their idea maps. They can also add details to topics they listed previously. Topics might include space travel, Earth's environment, health, or natural resources.

5. **Read and Think**: Repeat the process, this time reading the next 12 pages, through the scene with the duck. This takes three to five minutes. Additional topics might include traffic, pollution, and animal habitats.

6. **Read and Think**: Repeat the process, reading the rest of the book. This takes three to five minutes. New topics might include feeling sorry or ashamed, making changes for the better, and trees.

7. **Group Presentations**: Give each group a few minutes to share its idea map. If possible, post the idea maps on a wall where students can see them during the rest of this lesson and the following lesson. Continue presentations the following day, if necessary.

8. **Lesson (for the next day)**: Explain that topics in a story work together to express a *theme*. A theme is a lesson or moral or an important insight (understanding) that the story teaches through the topics and details. Ask students to look at the idea maps they created as groups. Which topics have rich supporting examples in the story? How might these topics work together to express a theme? Ask volunteers to suggest themes. Examples might include, "We should take care of Earth" or "The future is what we make it." If students haven't suggested a theme using the topic of dreams, prompt them to do so by reminding them of the title of the book. A dream-related theme might be "Our dreams of the future can help us decide what to do in the present." Write examples of strong themes on a poster board that you can display on the wall.

9. **Wrap-Up**: Have students use information from the maps and the list of themes to write two-paragraph responses. In the first paragraph, they should identify two topics, along with supporting details, from *Just a Dream*. In the second paragraph, they

should identify a theme in *Just a Dream* and tell how the topics and details support, or reveal, that theme.

Differentiation

For students who need extra support

- Ask these students to be the scribes for their groups. As they write the topics and details, they are not under pressure to produce correct responses, but the physical act of writing correct responses will reinforce the concepts you are teaching. You can also monitor groups, affirming their construction of idea maps and asking leading questions.

For advanced students

- Ask these students to serve as spokespeople for their groups. As an added challenge, after a student presents the group's idea map, ask, "Is there anything you would add to or change in this idea map?"

Assessment

Use this rubric to assess the wrap-up writing activity. A top-score response earns 15 points.

Task	Choose One	Score
The student identifies two topics in the story.	novice: (1 point), proficient: (2 points), advanced: (3 points)	
The student supports each topic with details or examples from the story.	novice: (1 point), proficient: (2 points), advanced: (3 points)	
The student identifies a theme in the story.	novice: (1 point), proficient: (2 points), advanced: (3 points)	
The student explains how the topics and/or details support or reveal the theme.	novice: (1 point), proficient: (2 points), advanced: (3 points)	
The student gives topics, details, and a theme that accurately reflect the story.	novice: (1 point), proficient: (2 points), advanced: (3 points)	
	Total Points:	

Additional Resources

Other book or story pairs that work well in this and the following lesson are these:

- Versions of Cinderella from around the world, such as *Mufaro's Beautiful Daughters*, by John Steptoe; *The Irish Cinderlad*, *The Korean Cinderella*, and *The Persian Cinderella*, all by Shirley Climo; and *Fair, Brown, and Trembling*, by Jude Daly

- *Island of the Blue Dolphins*, by Scott O'Dell, and *Hatchet*, by Gary Paulsen. Choose a chapter or scene in each to compare, such as the scene in which the main character becomes stranded alone.
- *Jumanji* and *Zathura*, both by Chris Van Allsburg
- *Cloudy with a Chance of Meatballs* and *Pickles to Pittsburgh*, both by Judi Barrett (for younger grades)

Short and Long Vowel Sounds

Foundational Skills
Mini-Lesson

Common Core State Standards

4–5: Reading, Foundational Skills, Standard 3: Know and apply grade-level phonics and word analysis skills in decoding words. a. Use combined knowledge of all letter-sound correspondences, syllabication patterns, and morphology (e.g., roots and affixes) to accurately read unfamiliar words in context and out of context.

Planning and Preparation

- On a sheet of paper, list the following words in a numbered list. Next to each word, insert a write-on blank. Make copies for yourself and the students.

  Note: These words are from *Just a Dream*; you can select your own words based on your ongoing phonics instruction.

after	covers	friends	make	shrieking
back	deep	good-bye	medicine	throats
bought	doughnut	itch	overhead	through
breath	dream	kind	rocking	wait

- On a sheet of paper, create a word-sorting activity as follows: At the top, insert the following word bank, underlining syllables as shown. Below the word bank, list sorting categories with numbered write-on blanks: long *a* (2 blanks), short *a* (2 blanks), long *e* (3 blanks), short *e* (2 blanks), long *i* (2 blanks), short *i* (2 blanks), long *o* (3 blanks), short *o* (2 blanks), long *u* (1 blank), short *u* (1 blank). Make copies for yourself and the students.

<u>af</u>ter	<u>cov</u>ers	<u>friends</u>	<u>make</u>	<u>shriek</u>ing
<u>back</u>	<u>deep</u>	good-<u>bye</u>	me<u>di</u>cine	<u>throats</u>
<u>bought</u>	<u>dough</u>nut	<u>itch</u>	<u>o</u>verhead	<u>through</u>
<u>breath</u>	<u>dream</u>	<u>kind</u>	<u>rock</u>ing	<u>wait</u>

Agenda

1. Write the vowels on the board. Tell students that, as they know, English has five vowels. Let's say the vowels aloud together: *a, e, i, o, u.* Remind students that the sound they pronounce when they say a vowel aloud is the *long* vowel sound. Repeat the vowels aloud. Tell students that each vowel also has a *short* vowel sound. Say the short vowel sounds aloud, and then have students repeat the short sounds with you.

2. Pass out copies of the activity you prepared in the first item of the planning section. Tell students that each word has at least one short or long vowel sound. Point out the word *after.* Say, "In *after*, the letter *a* makes the short vowel sound." Point out the word *bought.* Say, "In *bought*, two vowels work together to make the short *o* sound." Read each word in the list aloud. After each word, have the class read the word aloud with you.

3. Ask students to fold their papers vertically and place them so that they can see only the numbered blanks. Read each word aloud. Students should write the word on the blank, spelling it as accurately as they can. Once students have spelled all the words, they can unfold their paper, check the correct spellings, and make corrections to their own work as needed.

4. Organize students into small groups, and pass out copies of the word-sorting activity sheet (second planning item). Point out that one syllable in each word in the word bank is underlined. Group members should read each word aloud and listen to the vowel sound in the underlined syllable. Then they should write the word on a blank line in the appropriate category. To model the activity, complete the process using one word.

5. As a class, review the word-sorting activity.

Assessment

- Check to make sure that students have correctly spelled each word in the spelling activity (self-corrections are acceptable). Mark words that are still incorrect, and ask students to try again.

- Collect the word-sorting activity completed as group work. Pass out fresh copies of the same activity and ask each student to complete the activity independently, either in class or for homework. ■

Notes

After implementing the lesson, make notes on what worked and what you would change next time.

_____

_____

_____

_____

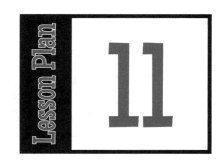

The Same—but Not Really!

Compare and Contrast Themes

Grade Levels: 4–5

Time Frame: Approximately one or two class periods

Overview: This lesson builds on the previous one by teaching students to compare and contrast themes in adventure stories. The assessment includes an essay assignment.

Common Core State Standards

- 4: Reading, Literature, Standard 9: Compare and contrast the treatment of similar themes and topics . . . in stories, myths, and traditional literature from different cultures.

- 5: Reading, Literature, Standard 9: Compare and contrast stories in the same genre (e.g., mysteries and adventure stories) on their approaches to similar themes and topics.

- 4–5: Writing, Standard 2: Write informative/explanatory texts to examine a topic and convey ideas and information clearly.

- 4: Writing, Standard 5: With guidance and support from peers and adults, develop and strengthen writing as needed by planning, revising, and editing.

- 5: Writing, Standard 5: With guidance and support from peers and adults, develop and strengthen writing as needed by planning, revising, editing, rewriting, or trying a new approach.

- 4–5: Writing, Standard 9: Draw evidence from literary or informational texts to support analysis, reflection, and research.

Objectives

- Students will identify topics and themes in an adventure story.

- Students will compare and contrast topics and themes in two adventure stories.

- Students will write essays comparing or contrasting themes in two adventure stories.

Background Knowledge Required

This lesson was designed to immediately follow Lesson 10, "A Special Message from the Author: Determine Topics and Theme in a Story."

Materials Needed

- Copy of *Just a Dream*, by Chris Van Allsburg, to review if necessary

- Copy of *Ben's Dream*, by Chris Van Allsburg, to read aloud

- Copies of a blank Venn diagram that you make or find online (optional)

Agenda

1. **Introduction**: Tell students that they will continue the discussion of topics and themes by comparing *Just a Dream* to another book by the same author.

2. **Read Aloud**: Read aloud the title, author, and all pages of *Ben's Dream*, showing the illustrations. This takes about five minutes.

3. **Group Work**: Organize students into small groups. Each group should create an idea map with the words *Topics in Ben's Dream* in the center circle. Students should jot down a few of the topics they identified in this story. Examples may include geography, friendship, dreams, and great landmarks of the world. Students should connect supporting details and examples to the topics.

4. **Full-Class Discussion**: Ask students to look at their idea maps about *Ben's Dream* and suggest a few themes that the ideas support. Examples might include "Dreams can take us anywhere" or "You can travel the world in your dreams." On a poster board, list strong themes that students suggest, and display the list for the remainder of the lesson.

   Note: You can break the lesson here, continuing on another day.

5. **Compare and Contrast**: Tell students that now you'd like them to compare *Just a Dream* and *Ben's Dream*.

   - On the board, draw a Venn diagram labeled Topics. Label one side Just a Dream and the other side Ben's Dream. Label the middle Both. Guide students to list topics that are the same and different in each book. Encourage students to take notes, either on their own paper or on copies of a blank Venn diagram you have passed out.
   - Draw another Venn diagram, labeling this one Themes. Label the sections as before. Guide students to list themes that are the same and different. If students haven't identified a theme that is the same, remind them that both books use the word *dream* in the title, and in both books, a boy travels in space. An example of a shared theme is "Dreams can take you anywhere." Again, make sure students take notes on their own paper or a blank Venn diagram you provide.

6. **Wrap-Up**: Ask students why authors might include themes in their stories. Possible answers may include "to give meaning to the story," "to help people see life differently," and "to teach people to do things in a better way."

Differentiation

For students who need extra support

- When assigning the group work activity, suggest a topic and supporting example to get students' ideas flowing. Group these students together so you can spend more time with them, affirming the construction of idea maps and asking leading questions.

For advanced students

- Group advanced students together to work on their idea maps, encouraging them to challenge one another to think deeply about the topics, examples, and themes.

Assessment

Ask students to write essays that compare or contrast a theme in *Just a Dream* and a theme in *Ben's Dream.* If students need extra support, devote a class period to guiding them through writing a simple essay in class. To help struggling students, you could create a shared outline as a class and then assign one paragraph to be written each night for homework. If students are more confident essay writers, the assignment works as an in-class or at-home writing assignment.

The essay should

- identify a theme in *Just a Dream*
- give details or examples from *Just a Dream* to explain the theme
- identify a theme in *Ben's Dream*
- give details or examples from *Ben's Dream* to explain the theme
- tell how the two themes are alike or different.

Remind students to use details and examples from their idea maps to help support their ideas in the essay. Use the following rubric, or one you design, to assess the essays.

Score 4.0	The student • Identifies a theme in each book. • Gives details and examples from each book to explain the book's theme. • Tells clearly how the themes are alike or different. • Expresses ideas in sentences using legible handwriting. No major errors or omissions in the score 4.0 content.
Score 3.5	The student demonstrates success at the 3.0 level plus partial success at the 4.0 level.
Score 3.0	The student • Identifies a theme in each book. • Gives details from one book to explain a theme. • States that the themes are alike or different. • Expresses ideas mostly in sentences using legible handwriting. No major errors or omissions in the score 3.0 content.
Score 2.5	The student demonstrates success at the 2.0 level plus partial success at the 3.0 level.
Score 2.0	The student • Identifies a theme in one of the books. • States that the themes are alike or different. • Expresses ideas using complete and incomplete sentences. No major errors or omissions in the score 2.0 content.

Score 1.5	The student demonstrates partial success at the 2.0 level. The student may confuse theme with topic but attempts to meet the essay requirements anyway.
Score 1.0	With help, the student achieves partial success at score 2.0 and 3.0 contents. Responses are simplistic and limited; explanations and examples may be unclear.
Score 0.5	With help, the student achieves partial success at score 2.0 content but not score 3.0 content.
Score 0.0	Even with help, the student has no success.

Additional Resources

See Additional Resources in Lesson 10 for a list of other book or story pairs that work well in Lessons 10 and 11.

Syllabication Patterns

> **Foundational Skills Mini-Lesson**

Common Core State Standards

4–5: Reading, Foundational Skills, Standard 3: Know and apply grade-level phonics and word analysis skills in decoding words. a. Use combined knowledge of all letter-sound correspondences, syllabication patterns, and morphology (e.g., roots and affixes) to read accurately unfamiliar multisyllabic words in context and out of context.

Planning and Preparation

- Review the syllabication rules listed in agenda item 3. Choose one or more rules to teach today.

- Based on the rules you are teaching today, prepare a work sheet that lists words for students to divide into syllables. Suggested words, drawn from *Ben's Dream* and *Just a Dream*, are listed for most rules. Make copies for yourself and the students.

Agenda

1. Tell students that all words are made up of one or more syllables and that a *syllable* is a single speech sound made up of a vowel sound with or without a consonant sound. Ask, "What does *every* syllable have to have?" (a vowel sound) "What might or might not be in a syllable?" (a consonant sound)

2. Say, "Here is an example of a word divided into syllables: ge/og/ra/phy. How many syllables does this word have?" (four) "What is the vowel sound in each syllable?" Read each syllable aloud, pointing out the vowel sound. Explain that the letter *y* sometimes works as a vowel. "Does each syllable have a consonant sound?" Yes. Point out that in the last syllable, the letters *ph* work together to make one consonant sound.

3. Tell students that English has some rules to help readers divide words into syllables accurately. Introduce one or more of the following rules, saving the others for another day.

- Divide a compound word into the words that form it (e.g., *drive/way*). Then, divide each word if necessary (e.g., *a/maze/ment*). Continue with other words: *landmarks, baseball, downpour, sunshine, sleepyhead, outside, doughnut, birthday, understand.*
- Prefixes and suffixes usually form separate syllables (e.g., *light/ly*). Other words: *sleepy, floated, waving, quickly.*
- Two identical consonants are divided when they are between vowels (e.g., *jel/ly*). Other words: *tomorrow, dinner, button.*
- Do not split two vowels that work together to make one sound (e.g., *peo/ple*). Additional examples: *floated, neutral, around, thousand.*
- Divide syllables between vowels that make separate sounds. Look at the first and second syllables of *ge/og/ra/phy.*
- A single consonant between two vowels goes with the first vowel if the first vowel is short and is accented (e.g., *ped/al*). (You could explain that an *accented* vowel is one that we say stronger or louder than another one nearby.) Other words: *very, gravel, never, present, busy.* It goes with the second vowel if the first vowel is long (e.g., *be/cause*). Other words: *began, open, robot, future.*
- Two or more consonants between vowels go with the second vowel if the first vowel is long (e.g., *be/tween*). They are divided if the first vowel is short (e.g., *crum/ple*). Other words: *window, under, fingers, garbage, distant.* They are not divided if they form a blended sound (e.g., *moth/er*). Other words: *father, rhythmic, empty, hydrant, machine.*

4. Organize students into groups, and have them complete the work sheet you prepared, dividing each word into its syllables.

5. As a full class, review the work sheets, reminding students of the rule that applies to each example.

Assessment

Collect the work sheets that students completed as group work. Pass out fresh copies of the same work sheet for students to complete independently, either in class or for homework. Evaluate students' work to see how well they are retaining knowledge of syllabication patterns. ■

Notes

After implementing the lesson, make notes on what worked and what you would change next time.

_____

_____

_____

_____

Prove It to Me!

Identify Supporting Reasons

Grade Levels: 4–5

Time Frame: Approximately one or two class periods

Overview: This lesson uses a short yet complex science text about Mars to show how an author uses evidence to support a point. You may want to adapt the lesson to a science or social studies text that students are reading for class. An opinion text would work as well.

Common Core State Standards

- 4: Reading, Informational Text, Standard 8: Explain how an author uses reasons and evidence to support particular points in a text.

- 5: Reading, Informational Text, Standard 8: Explain how an author uses reasons and evidence to support particular points in a text, identifying which reasons and evidence support which point(s).

- 4–5: Language, Standard 6: Acquire and use accurate, grade-appropriate general academic and domain-specific words and phrases.

Objectives

- Students will comprehend a short yet complex science text.

- Students will identify points the author makes.

- Students will identify reasons and facts that support a particular point in the text.

Background Knowledge Required

No particular background knowledge is required for this lesson.

Materials Needed

- Copies of "Is There Life on Mars?": coolcosmos.ipac.caltech.edu/cosmic_kids/AskKids/marslife.shtml

- Dictionaries or encyclopedias (one per group of students; see Agenda item 3)

- Copies of the handout: Author's Point and Evidence Activity Sheet, p. 78

Agenda

1. **Introduction**: Introduce the topic of Mars and the question the article poses. You could say something such as, "Let's talk about Mars! You know what Mars is, right?" Pause to let students identify it as a planet, the red planet, etc. "Well, have you ever wondered if there is life on Mars?" Pause to let students say yes, no, or that they already know the answer to this question. "Let's see what scientists have to tell us about life on Mars."

2. **Read Aloud**: Pass out copies of the article. Ask students to follow along as you read aloud, or ask students to take turns reading sentences until the article has been read completely.

3. **Vocabulary Activity**: Tell students, "This is a scientific article. It uses a lot of words from the field of science. These science words help the writer give information accurately. Let's go through the article and make sure we all understand these keywords from science." Ask students to read the article independently, underlining any words they don't understand. Have students help you create a master list of Words to Know on the board. Organize students into small groups, pass out dictionaries or encyclopedias, and have each group find and write down an explanation of one or more words. Finally, have the groups report back to the class.

4. **Modeling Activity**: Explain that articles such as this one do two things. They state facts and ideas, and they give evidence to support the facts and ideas. Evidence is the details, reasons, and examples that support a point. In other words, the author makes a *point* and gives *evidence* to support the point. The first sentence in the article makes a point—"This is a question which scientists and others have been asking for a long time"—and then gives evidence to support, or show the truth of, the point—"because Mars is more similar to Earth than any other planet in the solar system."

5. **Guided Practice**: Ask students to underline the clause "Mars is more similar to Earth than any other planet in the solar system." Explain that the author used this fact to support the first point in the article. But the author also supports this fact, or point, with evidence. Ask students to read the next sentence, beginning with "There is also evidence . . . , " and identify two pieces of evidence the author gives to support the point that they underlined. Answers: Water once flowed on Mars in the past, and there is frozen water on Mars. Explain again that authors of informational texts make points and then support the points with evidence. The job of readers is to identify points and connect them to evidence.

   Note: You can break the lesson here, continuing on another day.

6. **Independent Practice**: Ask students to underline the sentence "Spacecraft have been sent. . . . " On their own, students should identify three details that support the author's point in this sentence. The answers are in the three sentences that follow the one they just underlined. As a full class, review students' work.

7. **Wrap-Up**: Pass out the handout and another short text from the Ask an Astronomer for Kids website, such as "Are there really black holes in space?": coolcosmos.ipac .caltech.edu/cosmic_kids/AskKids/blackhole_space.shtml. Have students use the text to complete the handout.

Extend the Lesson

Pass out copies of the handout. Have students use what they learned in the lesson to complete the entire handout. Then have students use the handout to help them write paragraphs that answer the question "Is there life on Mars?" The paragraphs should

- make a point—yes, there is life, or no, there isn't life
- give evidence to support the point. Remind students that if they borrow words from the article, they must enclose them in quotation marks.

Differentiation

For students who need extra support

- Type a second copy of the article. Instead of grouping sentences as a paragraph, list each sentence separately. This will help students focus on one idea at a time and make it easier to see a list of details that follows a point that you underline during the lesson.

For advanced students

- In the vocabulary activity, assign advanced students to be spokespeople for their groups, or, instead of having students work in groups, ask volunteers to consult a reference source and read a word's definition to the entire class. Call on a different volunteer for each domain-specific word.

Assessment

Use this rubric to assess the wrap-up activity.

Score	The student
4	• Identifies a point that the author is making. • Identifies two or three pieces of evidence that logically connect to the author's point.
3	• Identifies a point that the author is making. • Identifies one or two logical pieces of evidence. • May identify a fact or detail that does not logically support the author's point.
2	• Identifies a point that the author is making. OR • Identifies one logical piece of supporting evidence. • Identifies a fact or detail that does not logically support the author's point.
1	• Identifies a point that the author is making. • Identifies unconnected ideas as the author's point and supporting reasons.
0	• Identifies unconnected ideas as the author's point and supporting reasons.

Additional Resources

By using the search term *main idea supporting details graphic organizer* to search for images in an Internet browser, you can find numerous—and creative—graphic organizers that will work with this lesson.

┌─────────────────┐
│ Foundational Skills │
│   Mini-Lesson   │
└─────────────────┘

Prefixes and Suffixes

Common Core State Standards

4–5: Reading, Foundational Skills, Standard 3: Know and apply grade-level phonics and word analysis skills in decoding words. a. Use combined knowledge of all letter-sound correspondences, syllabication patterns, and morphology (e.g., roots and affixes) to read accurately unfamiliar multisyllabic words in context and out of context.

Planning and Preparation

No special preparation is needed for this mini-lesson.

Agenda

1. Remind students that a prefix is a word part added to the beginning of a word to make a new word. To review, write the word *displace* on the board. Ask a volunteer to identify the prefix in *displace*. Ask students to speculate on what *dis-* means (apart, away, the reverse). Ask a few volunteers to give examples of what might cause people to be *displaced* (e.g., a hurricane, a fire, a war). Depending on students' answers, you may need to distinguish between *dis-* and *mis-* (mistaken, wrong, incorrectly). Something that is displaced is not necessarily misplaced. People might misplace their keys, but if a wildfire drives them from their homes, they are displaced, not misplaced.

2. Remind students that a suffix is a word part added to the end of a word to make a new word. To review, write the word *metallic* on the board. Ask a volunteer to identify the suffix. Write *metal* + *-ic* on the board. Point out that *metal* is a noun, but *metallic* is an adjective. The suffix *-ic* is used to make an adjective form of a word. Point out that we double the *l* in *metal* when we add the suffix *-ic*. A spelling rule tells us that when a word ends in a single vowel followed by a single consonant, then we double the consonant before adding a suffix beginning with a vowel (e.g., *shopping*, *biggest*). Ask a few volunteers to give examples of what might be *metallic* (e.g., earrings, nail clippers, car door, scissors, etc.).

3. Tell students that prefixes and suffixes can be added to a base word, such as *place* or *metal*. They may also be added to a *root*, which cannot stand alone as a word. Break down the word *astronomer* to show the prefix *astro-* (meaning "having to do with stars or other celestial bodies or activities that take place outside Earth's atmosphere), the suffix *-er* (meaning "one who"; it creates a noun form), and the root *nom* (meaning "law" or "order").

4. Organize students into small groups. Ask them to use their knowledge of prefixes, suffixes, and roots to understand and answer the following questions. You may want to create your own questions, related to or drawn from a science or social studies text in your curriculum.

   - What does an astronomer most likely study?
   - Where would an astronaut go to do his or her job?

- Do you think an astrodome would be located on the top or the bottom of an aircraft? Why?
- Where does an astrotourist go on vacation?
- The prefix *auto-* means "self." Based on your knowledge of *auto-* and *nom*, which sentence do you think uses *autonomy* correctly?
  If you promise to follow the rules, you can have your autonomy at the party.
  Students at my school show autonomy by riding the school bus together.
- What is one thing your parents, coach, or teacher disapproves of?
- What would a person more likely want to dispel—a bad mood or a good mood?
- Suppose an evil fairy enchanted a prince and turned him into a frog. If you figured out how to disenchant the frog, what would happen?
- If you combine *general* with *-ic* to form *generic*, what could you describe with your new adjective?
- Where could you read about a mythic hero?

Assessment

As groups work on the written activity, monitor their answers. If students are struggling, go over the questions as a class and ask volunteers to share their answers.
You could also assign just five of the questions as group work and the other five for homework or a quiz. Be sure to include a usage of *nom*, *dis-*, and *-ic* in each set of five questions.   ■

Notes

After implementing the lesson, make notes on what worked and what you would change next time.

_____

_____

_____

_____

Name: _____   Date: _____

Author's Point and Evidence Activity Sheet

Part 1: *Use this organizer to show how an author uses reasons, details, or examples to support a point.*

Title of article: _____

Author of article: _____

In the article, the author makes this point:

_____

_____

The author supports the point with this reason, fact, or example:	The author supports the point with this reason, fact, or example:	The author supports the point with this reason, fact, or example:

Part 2: Use the information that you wrote in the organizer to fill in the outline below.

I.   Author's point: _____

_____

    A. Evidence: _____

    B. Evidence: _____

    C. Evidence: _____

Writing

Overview

According to the Common Core State Standards, narrative writing is still important in elementary school; however, opinion-based and expository writing need to be included too. The standards say that in grades K–5, 30 percent of writing should be to argue, 35 percent should be to explain/inform, and 35 percent should be narrative writing. Don't forget that genres do overlap; for example, argument writing will have to include information. The standards also emphasize the importance of teaching research skills, teaching students to use technology—during the writing process and to publish writing—and showing students how to collaborate with peers and adults to edit writing as needed. For more tips for revising your lessons or creating new ones, read the checklist below.

Planning Checklist

When planning a CCSS-based writing lesson, keep the following tips in mind.

☐ Teach students to consider task, purpose, and audience when writing. Students shouldn't just write to the teacher as their audience but should write in both formal and informal contexts. Give students a variety of audiences so they learn to adapt their language accordingly.

☐ Have students brainstorm, revise, and edit their writing with partners, in small groups, and one-on-one with the teacher. Also give students tools to become independent at checking their own writing. For example, use checklists and rubrics, and give them to students while they're writing, not just at the end when you're ready to assess them.

☐ Use mentor texts to teach all genres of writing. Point out the effective features of those texts but allow students to make their own discoveries about those texts.

☐ Teach grammar in the context of writing. For more on how to do so, see the lesson plans on pages 176 and 181 of this book.

☐ Incorporate technology into your writing lessons. For example, young students can contribute to a class wiki to gather ideas, or they can publish their writing on a class blog, or enter an online writing contest for their age group. For a lesson plan on teaching blogging, see page 114 of this book. Make sure you teach students how to be safe and responsible on the web.

☐ Teach students how (and when) to conduct online research. Students need to learn that they can't just google a topic and trust the first site that comes up. Show students how to use good search terms, how to sort their search results, and how to determine whether a website is helpful, based on their information needs. Also show students how (and why) to quote or paraphrase information. Teach about plagiarism and how to avoid it early. Citing sources: Students in grades K–5 can just make a list of their sources; they are not required by the standards to learn proper MLA citation formatting until grades 6 and up.

☐ Teach opinion-based writing (called argument writing in grades 6–12). Show students how to gather reasons and evidence for their opinion-based writing. You may wish to use sentence or paragraph frames with students to give them some preliminary structure for their writing.

☐ Teach transition (linking) words to help students with informational and opinion-based writing.

☐ Feel free to teach additional genres such as poetry. The standards do not explicitly mention poetry as a genre of writing. However, that doesn't mean you can't teach it. Appendix A of the standards provides the following clarification: "The narrative category does not include all of the possible forms of creative writing, such as many types of poetry. The Standards leave the inclusion and evaluation of other such forms to teacher discretion" (The Common Core State Standards, Appendix A, p. 23).

Lesson Plans at a Glance

And What Happened Next?

Write a Narrative

Grade Levels: K–1

Time Frame: Approximately two class periods

Overview: This lesson covers the foundational skills of writing a narrative. It first has students retell a story that they listened to, focusing on putting events in order. Then students move on to telling their original stories, again with an emphasis on putting events in a logical order.

Common Core State Standards

- K: Writing, Standard 3: Use a combination of drawing, dictating, and writing to narrate a single event or several loosely linked events, tell about the events in the order in which they occurred, and provide a reaction to what happened.

- 1: Writing, Standard 3: Write narratives in which they recount two or more appropriately sequenced events, include some details regarding what happened, use temporal words to signal event order, and provide some sense of closure.

- K: Reading, Literature, Standard 2: With prompting and support, retell familiar stories, including key details.

- 1: Reading, Literature, Standard 2: Retell familiar stories, including key details, and demonstrate understanding of their central message or lesson.

Objectives

- Using drawing and writing, students will retell a sequence of events from a story they listened to.

- Using drawing and writing, students will tell a sequence of events in an original story.

Background Knowledge Required

No particular background knowledge is required for this lesson.

Materials Needed

- An audio story or a storybook to read aloud

- Copies of the handout: Write a Story Activity Sheet, p. 87

Agenda

1. **Introduction**: Engage students' interest in stories by asking a few warm-up questions, such as "How many of you like to read stories?" "Do you like to tell stories about fun things that happened?" "Who is one of your favorite story characters?" "What did that character do in a story?"

2. **Listening Activity**: Have students listen to the audio story or to you as you read a story aloud.

3. **Guided Writing Activity**: Pass out the handout. Tell students to think about the story that they heard. What happened at the beginning of the story? What happened in the middle? What happened at the end? Tell them they don't need to answer aloud but should think about the questions so they can complete the activity. Then ask them to look at the handout. Read aloud the writing prompt in each quadrant. Point out the numbers, 1 through 4. Tell students that they will retell the story that they heard. Explain that they need to retell the beginning, middle, and end in order. Kindergarteners can rely on drawing the scenes in order and, if they are able, writing a short sentence in each quadrant. First graders should draw a scene and write a sentence in each quadrant.

4. **Independent Writing Activity** (next lesson period): Pass out fresh copies of the handout. Tell students that today, they will write their own stories. They can use their imaginations to make up characters for the story. They can make up what happens in the story. Help students get their ideas flowing by asking questions such as, "If you were a princess (or superhero), what kind of adventure do you think you would have?" or "If you went to the beach today, what kind of adventure would you have?" Review the four quadrants of the handout, reminding students that events in a story happen in order: "first," "next," "after that," and "at the end." Have students complete the handout as they did in the guided writing activity.

5. **Wrap-Up**: For homework, have students read their stories to parents or guardians at home.

Extend the Lesson

- Have students use their work to create mini-books. First, they should cut out each quadrant. Next, they should arrange the pages in order. After that, they should write titles and their names on the covers (you could provide pre-cut pieces of construction paper). Finally, they should get your help stapling the books.

- Have students write a third story, this time focusing on one aspect of the writer's craft, such as showing, not telling (e.g., "Huff! Puff!" said Wolf vs. The wolf blew really hard.) For more ideas on the writer's craft, see Glorianne Bradshaw's article listed in additional resources.

Differentiation

For students who need extra support

- In advance of the lesson, complete a model of the handout. Use it as a visual while you explain the assignment, and display it for students to refer to as they complete their work.

For advanced students

- Encourage students to include a detail about the setting (place, weather, time of day, etc.) in each quadrant.

Assessment

Evaluate each story to see that students placed events in sequence. Here is a useful rubric. A top score is 12.

Task	Choose One	Score
The student tells events in order.	novice: (1 point), proficient: (2 points), advanced: (3 points)	
The student identifies a scene that gives closure to the story.	novice: (1 point), proficient: (2 points), advanced: (3 points)	
The student identifies one or more characters in the story.	novice: (1 point), proficient: (2 points), advanced: (3 points)	
The student uses words or sentences to help tell the story.	novice: (1 point), proficient: (2 points), advanced: (3 points)	
	Total Points:	

Additional Resources

Glorianne Bradshaw's "The How of Writing: First-Graders Learn Craft" explains how she uses Arnold Lobel's Frog and Toad books to teach aspects of a writer's craft: sentence modeling, show not tell, onomatopoeia, and "good beginnings." The National Writing Project published her article here: www.nwp.org/cs/public/print/resource/2188.

Notes

After implementing the lesson, make notes on what worked and what you would change next time.

Write a Story Activity Sheet

1. First, this happened.	**2.** Next, this happened.
3. After that, this happened.	**4.** At the end, this happened.

This Is What I Think

Write an Opinion

Lesson Plan 14

Grade Levels: K–1; can be adapted to older grades (see note in Overview)

Time Frame: Approximately two or three class periods

Overview: This lesson introduces the concept of opinion, distinguishing it from fact and story. It asks students to use a combination of drawing, copying, and writing to express opinions and give reasons for their opinions. For kindergartners, you may wish to omit the part of the lesson that covers reasons. You can adapt the lesson to older grades by teaching additional opinion words and linking the writing activity to writing a paragraph instead of drawing a picture.

Common Core State Standards

- K: Writing, Standard 1: Use a combination of drawing, dictating, and writing to compose opinion pieces in which they tell a reader the topic or the name of the book they are writing about and state an opinion or preference about the topic or book (e.g., *My favorite book is . . .*).

- 1: Writing, Standard 1: Write opinion pieces in which they introduce the topic or name the book they are writing about, state an opinion, supply a reason for the opinion, and provide some sense of closure.

- K: Language, Standard 1: Demonstrate command of the conventions of standard English grammar and usage when writing or speaking. a. Print many upper- and lowercase letters.

- 1: Language, Standard 1: Demonstrate command of the conventions of standard English, grammar, and usage when writing or speaking. a. Print all upper- and lowercase letters.

- K: Language, Standard 6: Use words and phrases acquired through conversations, reading and being read to, and responding to texts.

- 1: Language, Standard 6: Use words and phrases acquired through conversations, reading and being read to, and responding to texts, including frequently occurring conjunctions to signal simple relationships (e.g., *because*).

Objectives

- Students will learn what an opinion is.

- Students will write an opinion statement.

- Students will give one reason to support an opinion.

- Students will use opinion words (e.g., *best, favorite*) and reason words (e.g., *because*).

- Students will use drawings to help express opinions.

Background Knowledge Required

No particular background knowledge is required for this lesson.

Materials Needed

- Copies of the handout: Opinion Activity Sheet, p. 92

- Copies of the handout: Opinion with Reason Activity Sheet, p. 93

Agenda

1. **Introduction**: Help students discover what an opinion is and how it differs from a fact and a story. You might use the concept of pets and talk about what a pet is (fact) and then ask a volunteer to tell you how he or she takes care of a pet (story). Then tell students that people can talk about pets by giving their *opinions*. You might say, "An opinion is what someone thinks about something. Other people might think something different. For example, 'Alligators make the best pets.' Who agrees with this? Who does not agree with this? What do you think is the best pet? Good! You have just told me an opinion."

   On the board, write the sentences "The best pet is _____ ." and "The worst pet is _____ ." Underline the word *best* and explain that it is an opinion word. This word helps a speaker or writer give an opinion. So does *worst*. Demonstrate by writing two model sentences of your own, using extreme examples that students will find it easy to disagree with. For example, "The best pet is an elephant" and "The worst pet is a goldfish."

   Pass out the Opinion Activity Sheet. Have students draw pictures of *either* the best pet or the worst pet, in their opinion. On the lines, students should write a sentence to express their opinion about the best or worst pet. Remind them to refer to the model sentences on the board to get help with spelling and wording.

2. **Continue the Lesson** (next class period): Briefly review the concept of opinion by writing model sentences on the board. Choose a new topic (instead of pets), such as a favorite snack. Point out the opinion word *favorite*, and remind students that opinion words help people give their opinions. Then explain that people can give *reasons* for their opinions. A reason tells people why that is someone's opinion. Give examples. "My favorite snack is string cheese because it is fun to eat." Underline *because*, and explain that this word helps a person give a reason for his or her opinion.

   Pass out the Opinion with Reason Activity Sheet. Have students draw pictures of their favorite snacks. On the lines, students should write a sentence or two. They should tell what their favorite snacks are (opinion) and give reasons. Remind students to refer to the model sentences on the board to get help with spelling and wording.

3. **Wrap-Up**: Collect the completed activity sheets. Hold up and read aloud each one, emphasizing the opinion word (*favorite*) and the reason word (*because*). If a student's

work doesn't express an opinion and/or a reason, just read it and go on. You can provide constructive feedback in the assessment activity.

Extend the Lesson

Ask students to browse the classroom library and choose a favorite book. Pass out fresh copies of the Opinion Activity Sheet or the Opinion with Reason Activity Sheet and have them write a sentence(s) to tell what their favorite book is about and, if required, a reason for the opinion. For example, "My favorite book is about volcanoes because I can see a real one." Then they should draw a picture of what the book is about (e.g., a volcano).

Differentiation

For students who need extra support
- Prepare activity sheets that have fill-in-the-blank sentences to express the opinion and the reason. Ask students to underline the opinion word and the reason word in their completed sentences.

For advanced students
- Give the option of writing two reasons to support an opinion.

Assessment

- Meet with students in small groups to review their Opinion Activity Sheets. Ask each student to read his or her opinion. Affirm that it is an opinion ("Good. You told me what you think the *worst* pet is. That is your opinion.") or give corrective feedback ("You told me a fact: 'I love my cat.' That is not an opinion. Would you say that a cat makes the *best* or the *worst* pet? OK, write that down: 'A cat is the best pet.' That is your *opinion*. Do you see the opinion word that you used, *best*?"

- Review the Opinion with Reason Activity Sheets, giving feedback to affirm or correct responses. "Emily, let's talk about what you wrote. What is your favorite snack? Good. That is your *opinion*: 'My favorite snack is a cookie.' Can you tell me *why* a cookie is your favorite snack? Good! That is the *reason* for your opinion 'It tastes good.'" or "Lyle, would you read your sentence to me? What you read is a story. It tells me that you ate pizza. Is pizza your favorite snack? OK, take this sheet of paper. Write a sentence that tells me that pizza is your *favorite* snack. Good. Do you see the opinion word that you used? You wrote an opinion. Now, can you tell me *why* pizza is your favorite snack? Great! That is a *reason* for your opinion. Write that down. Now you have written an opinion and a reason for the opinion. Nice work!"

Additional Resources

- ReadWorks has a kindergarten lesson on forming and writing opinions using sentence starters: www.readworks.org/lessons/gradek/fact-and-opinion/lesson-1.

- ReadWorks has a first-grade lesson on identifying opinions with signal words: www.readworks.org/lessons/grade1/fact-and-opinion/lesson-1.

Notes

After implementing the lesson, make notes on what worked and what you would change next time.

_____

_____

_____

_____

Name: _____   Date: _____

Opinion Activity Sheet

```
┌──────────────────────────────────────────────────┐
│                                                    │
│                                                    │
│                                                    │
│                                                    │
│                                                    │
│                                                    │
│                                                    │
│                                                    │
│                                                    │
│                                                    │
└──────────────────────────────────────────────────┘
```

_____

_____

_____

_____

_____

Opinion with Reason Activity Sheet

Great Topics!

Research to Learn More

Grade Levels: 2–3

Time Frame: Approximately three class periods

Overview: This lesson teaches students to consider a range of topics for a research project, to narrow the topics down to one, to identify research goals, to consult print and digital sources to answer questions, and to take research notes. Though it is ambitious, this lesson guides students through the process step-by-step. Much of the work is shared in small groups. This lesson is designed to be used in conjunction with Lesson Plan 16, "That's a Fact! Write an Informative Text."

Common Core State Standards

- 2: Writing, Standard 7: Participate in shared research and writing projects (e.g., read a number of books on a single topic to produce a report; record science observations).

- 3: Writing, Standard 7: Conduct short research projects that build knowledge about a topic.

- 2: Writing, Standard 8: Recall information from experiences or gather information from provided sources to answer a question.

- 3: Writing, Standard 8: Recall information from experiences or gather information from print and digital sources; take brief notes on sources and sort evidence into provided categories.

- 3: Writing, Standard 10: Write routinely over extended time frames (time for research, reflection, and revision) and shorter time frames (a single sitting or a day or two) for a range of discipline-specific tasks, purposes, and audiences.

Objectives

- Students will work in small groups to conduct shared research projects.

- Students will research print and digital sources to find information on topics.

- Students will take notes on their research topics.

Background Knowledge Required

Students should know the difference between a text that tells a story and a text that gives information.

Materials Needed

- A selection of nonfiction texts, including books, magazines, and webpage printouts, on a variety of topics. Ideas include plants (how seeds grow), biography (e.g., Ruby Bridges), water, traveling to the moon, a planet, weather events, horses, and kangaroos. Gather enough texts so that each student in class can choose one to examine independently.

- Copies of the handout: Topic Activity Sheet, p. 98

- Copies of the handout: Note-Taking Sheet, p. 99

Agenda

1. **Introduction**: Set up a display of informational texts. Ask each student to browse the selections and choose one that interests him or her. Give everyone time to skim the texts. Meanwhile, on the board, write Reasons to Research a Topic. Ask students to help you make a list of reasons. Examples are to learn about a topic of interest and to find information to answer a question.

2. **Topic Activity**: As a class, create a Great Topics to Learn About list. Have students suggest topics that they could write informational reports on. Students should use the model texts to generate ideas for the list; it's OK if they simply volunteer the topics of the texts they have examined.

    Organize students into small groups. Pass out copies of the topic activity sheet. Have students complete the handout as groups. Remind students that the topic their group chose will be their shared research topic for the rest of the lesson.

3. **Resources Activity** (next class period): Review the kinds of resources that students might use to research their topics. Use this opportunity to teach about new resources, if needed. Ideas include classroom library, school library, public library, Internet (World Wide Web), informational DVDs, and interviews. Explain that students may need to consult different resources to find information to answer their research questions.

4. **Research Activity**: Explain that groups will divide the research tasks among the group members. Have students meet with their research groups. Each student should select one bullet item from the "What I Want to Know" section of the topic activity sheet. This item will be the student's personal research topic.

    Pass out copies of the note-taking sheet. Allow groups time to perform shared or independent research of their topics. For example, you could coordinate with the school librarian to have one group at a time gather resources in the school library. Likewise, you could coordinate with the computer teacher to assist one group at a time in finding one or two useful Web articles. You could take a field trip to a public library, coordinating with a librarian there. If a field trip isn't possible, consider sending home research notes that ask adults to help children find one or two useful books in a local or home library. Important: Have students check out or print the informational texts to share in class.

5. **Wrap-Up** (next class period): Have each group meet to go over its findings. Each group member should share his or her note-taking sheet. Then have each group show and briefly explain its resources to the class. For example, "This is a book about

tigers. One chapter tells about white tigers. It tells why some tigers are white and black instead of orange and black."

Extend the Lesson

Conduct a mini-lesson on how to copy and use a direct quotation from a source.

Differentiation

For students who need extra support

- Meet with individuals or groups to make sure that the "What I Want to Know" topics are narrow enough to facilitate success during the students' research.

For advanced students

- Ask volunteers to serve as spokespeople for their groups. Articulating the research findings challenges these students to think concretely about the purposes of using sources while providing a model thought process for struggling students.

Assessment

Evaluate students' note-taking sheets for completion, accuracy, and relevancy. Meet with struggling students to provide specific guidance if needed. You can assign a grade based on a 4-point scale using the following rubric.

Points to Earn	Task
1	Identifies a focused topic of research.
0.5	Records the text's title.
0.5	Records the text's author or creator.
1	Lists a relevant fact, definition, or example.
1	Lists a relevant fact, definition, or example (to total two pieces of evidence).
Top Score: 4	

Additional Resources

Too add variety to or change the focus of your lesson, you may want to review ideas in the following lessons on the ReadWriteThink website.

- "Using Web-Based Bookmarks to Conduct Internet Research": www.readwritethink .org/classroom-resources/lesson-plans/using-based-bookmarks-conduct-924.html

- "Creating Question and Answer Books through Guided Research": www .readwritethink.org/classroom-resources/lesson-plans/creating-question-answer -books-353.html

Notes

After implementing the lesson, make notes on what worked and what you would change next time.

_____

_____

_____

_____

Name: _____   Date: _____

Topic Activity Sheet

Write an answer to each question.

1. What are three topics that you would like to know more about?

   ▪ _____

   ▪ _____

   ▪ _____

2. Look at the topics you wrote in question 1. Which one do you *most* want to learn more about? Circle it.

3. Think about what you *already* know about the topic. Also think about what you *want* to know. Write some ideas in this chart.

What I Know	**What I Want to Know**
▪ _____ _____ ▪ _____ _____ ▪ _____ _____	▪ _____ _____ ▪ _____ _____ ▪ _____ _____

Note-Taking Sheet

1. My research topic is _____

_____

2. I found facts about my topic here:

Title of book or article: _____

Author's name or webpage creator's name: _____

3. Here is some helpful information about my topic. (Give facts, definitions, or examples.)

- _____

_____

- _____

_____

- _____

_____

That's a Fact!

Write an Informative Text

Grade Levels: 2–3

Time Frame: Approximately four class periods

Overview: This lesson guides students, step-by-step, through the process of writing a simple informational report. This lesson was designed to follow Lesson Plan 15, "Great Topics! Research to Learn More," in which students conducted a shared research project to gather notes on a topic.

Common Core State Standards

- 2: Writing, Standard 2: Write informative/explanatory texts in which they introduce a topic, use facts and definitions to develop points, and provide a concluding statement or section.

- 3: Writing, Standard 2: Write informative/explanatory texts to examine a topic and convey ideas and information clearly. a. Introduce a topic and group related information together; include illustrations when useful to aiding comprehension. b. Develop the topic with facts, definitions, and details. c. Use linking words and phrases (e.g., *also, another, and, more, but*) to connect ideas within categories of information. d. Provide a concluding statement or section.

- 2: Writing, Standard 5: With guidance and support from adults and peers, focus on a topic and strengthen writing as needed by revising and editing.

- 3: Writing, Standard 5: With guidance and support from peers and adults, develop and strengthen writing as needed by planning, revising, and editing.

Objectives

- Students will use notes they gathered previously to fill in graphic organizers and plan informational reports.

- Students will use their graphic organizers to write informational reports that include an introductory section, a body section, and a conclusion section.

- Students will revise their drafts to include linking words to connect ideas.

- Students will edit their drafts for capitalization, punctuation, and spelling conventions.

Background Knowledge Required

Students should know the difference between a text that tells a story and a text that gives information.

Materials Needed

- Students' note-taking sheets, completed in Lesson Plan 15

- Copies of the handout: Informational Report Planning Sheet, p. 105

Agenda

1. **Introduction**: Ask students to review the note-taking sheets they completed in the research lesson. Tell them that their research is valuable because now they can share what they learned with their own readers. But first, they need to write down the information so their classmates and others can read it. They will use their research notes to write informational reports. The reports will do three things: introduce a topic, give facts about the topic, and end with an important idea.

2. **Planning**: Explain that the first step in writing a report is to plan what goes into it. Pass out the handout. Have students use the information on their note-taking sheets to fill in their graphic organizers. Then have students meet with partners to share their graphic organizers. As they work independently and in pairs, move around, point out strengths, and make helpful suggestions, modeling the type of feedback that you would like students to learn to provide for one another.

3. **The Introductory Section** (next class period): Remind students that people read informational texts to learn about topics. Use the example of writing a report. The first thing a report should do is tell what the main topic is. If your students are ready to learn about and write paragraphs, you can explain that this section of the report is the introductory paragraph. Either way, as an example, you could read the introductory paragraph from an informational leveled reader.

   Next, have students look at their note-taking sheets. Ask students to write their topics at the top of fresh sheets of paper. These will be the titles of their reports. Then they should look at the introduction section of their Informational Report Planning Sheets. Using their planning work, they should write the first parts of their reports. At the end of the work period, ask a few volunteers to read their writing aloud, or collect students' work and choose a few to read yourself.

4. **The Body Section** (next class period): Tell students that the next part of their reports will give facts and details about their topics. Read a sample body paragraph from the leveled reader, pointing out how it gives facts, definitions, or details to help make the topic clear. Review the terms (*fact*, etc.) if necessary.

   Ask students to read the introduction they wrote previously. Then they should refer to their Informational Report Planning Sheets to write sentences (or a paragraph, if students are working in paragraphs) to give facts, definitions, or details to help make their topics clear.

   After students have written their first drafts, explain how they can use linking words such as *also, another, and, more,* and *but* to connect ideas. Have them go back to their drafts and insert one or two linking words to link ideas. Finally, have volunteers read their work or read samples aloud yourself.

5. **The Conclusion Section** (next class period): Briefly review the concepts of a report's introduction and body, reminding students that they have written much of their reports already. Encourage students to feel a sense of accomplishment for this work. Now it is time to give their reports endings. What goes in an ending? If an introduction asked a question, the writer should answer the question. The writer might provide an interesting fact or detail to help readers remember the main topic. The writer could tell readers why the information is important. As a model, read aloud the last paragraph of the leveled reader.

    Have students read what they have written so far and review their Informational Report Planning Sheets. Based on this information, they should write endings for their reports.

6. **Wrap-Up**: Have students edit their drafts. Provide a checklist based on your ongoing language instruction, such as checking for complete sentences, capital letters to begin sentences, end punctuation for sentences, and correct spelling.

Extend the Lesson

- Show students how to include direct quotations in their reports. You can do this in conjunction with writing the body section or as part of a mini-lesson on revising a draft to make it stronger.

- Have students draw or find illustrations that will help make their topics clear to their readers.

Differentiation

For students who need extra support

- After students have completed their Informational Report Planning Sheets, have them cut apart the planning boxes and glue each box at the top of separate sheets of paper. As you teach each section of the informational report, have students look at the relevant box and write the assigned text on the paper below it.

For advanced students

- Schedule class time for writing groups. Supply each group with a copy of a model introduction, body paragraph, or conclusion, depending on the focus for the day. Models can come from leveled readers or a sample you write at the students' reading levels. Appoint group leaders to read the model aloud to their groups. Each student should take a turn telling the group one thing that the model does well (e.g., "This sentence tells what the main topic is" or "This sentence gives an important fact about the topic"). Advanced students can model responses and assist others in interacting with the model text.

Assessment

Use this rubric to evaluate students' informational reports.

Score 4.0	The student
	▪ Introduces the topic he or she is writing about.
	▪ Develops the topic with three relevant facts, definitions, details, examples, or quotations.
	▪ Uses at least two linking words to connect related ideas.
	▪ Provides a concluding statement or section.
	▪ Makes few errors in the conventions listed in the lesson's editing activity.
	No major errors or omissions in the score 4.0 content.
Score 3.5	The student demonstrates success at the 3.0 level plus partial success at the 4.0 level.
Score 3.0	The student
	▪ Introduces the topic he or she is writing about.
	▪ Develops the topic with at least two relevant facts, definitions, details, examples, or quotations.
	▪ Uses at least one linking word to connect related ideas.
	▪ Provides a concluding statement or section.
	▪ Makes several errors in the conventions listed in the lesson's editing activity.
	No major errors or omissions in the score 3.0 content.
Score 2.5	The student demonstrates success at the 2.0 level plus partial success at the 3.0 level.
Score 2.0	The student
	▪ Introduces the topic he or she is writing about.
	▪ Develops the topic with at least one relevant fact, definition, or detail but may also include irrelevant information.
	▪ Provides a concluding statement or section, although it may merely repeat the information in the introductory section.
	▪ Makes numerous errors in the conventions listed in the lesson's editing activity.
	No major errors or omissions in the score 2.0 content.
Score 1.5	The student demonstrates partial success at the 2.0 level.
Score 1.0	With help, the student achieves partial success at score 2.0 and 3.0 contents.
Score 0.5	With help, the student achieves partial success at score 2.0 content but not score 3.0 content.
Score 0.0	Even with help, the student has no success.

Additional Resources

Using the search term *writing process posters printable* (or a similar term), you can search webpage images to find ideas or printables for visual aids to teaching this and other writing lessons. Teachers' blogs are useful sources for unique and practical classroom displays.

Notes

After implementing the lesson, make notes on what worked and what you would change next time.

_____

_____

_____

_____

Name: _____   Date: _____

Informational Report Planning Sheet

Plan what to write in your report by answering these questions.

1. What is the main topic of your report?

If your report answers a question, what is the question?

2. What fact, definition, or detail will help explain the topic?	**3.** What is another fact, definition, or detail that will help explain your topic?	**4.** What is another fact, definition, or detail that will help explain your topic?

5. What is the most important thing to remember about your topic?

If your introduction asked a question, what is the answer to the question?

What? Why? For Whom?

Consider Task, Purpose, and Audience

Grade Levels: 4–5

Time Frame: Approximately three class periods

Overview: This lesson introduces students to the academic terms *purpose, audience,* and *task* in connection with narrative, informative, and opinion texts. The lesson relies on a combination of instructional and group activities, culminating in the independent writing of informative/explanatory essays.

Common Core State Standards

- 4–5: Writing, Standard 4: Produce clear and coherent writing in which the development and organization are appropriate to task, purpose, and audience.

- 4–5: Writing, Standard 10: Write routinely over extended time frames (time for research, reflection, and revision) and shorter time frames (a single sitting or a day or two) for a range of discipline-specific tasks, purposes, and audiences.

- 4–5: Language, Standard 6: Acquire and accurately use grade-appropriate general academic and domain-specific words and phrases.

- 4–5: Speaking and Listening, Standard 1: Engage effectively in a range of collaborative discussions (one-on-one, in groups, and teacher-led) with diverse partners *on [grade-level] topics and texts,* building on others' ideas, and expressing their own clearly.

- 4: Reading, Informational Text, Standard 5: Describe the overall structure (e.g., chronology, comparison, cause/effect, problem/solution) of events, ideas, concepts, or information in a text or part of a text.

- 5: Reading, Informational Text, Standard 5: Compare and contrast the overall structure (e.g., chronology, comparison, cause/effect, problem/solution) of events, ideas, concepts, or information in two or more texts.

Objectives

- Students will examine model books to learn the terms *purpose, audience,* and *writer's task.*

- Students will work with peers to identify the purpose of, audience for, and method of organization of a model book.

- Students will work independently to develop, organize, and write an informative/ explanatory essay that meets stated requirements for purpose, audience, and writer's tasks.

Background Knowledge Required

Students should be familiar with three common text types: narratives, informative texts, and opinion texts; however, this lesson reviews these text types.

Materials Needed

- Two grade-level narratives, two grade-level informational texts, and two grade-level opinion texts. For the purposes of this lesson, books will work better than web-page printouts. Suggested books are Newbery Medal winners, biographies or science topics, and opinion-based books such as the You Wouldn't Want to Be books (e.g., *You Wouldn't Want to Be a Pyramid Builder,* written by Jacqueline Morely and illustrated by David Antram)

- Copies of the handout: Purpose, Audience, and Task Activity Sheet, p. 112

Agenda

1. **Introduction**: Set up a display of the books you selected. Introduce the idea of a text's purpose by saying something such as, "As you can see, books come in all shapes and sizes. These books are in print form, but you can also find books and articles in digital form, such as on an e-book reader or on the World Wide Web. No matter what form the text is in, it has a *purpose.* Every text was written for a purpose. Three common purposes for writing are these: to tell a story, to give information, and to explain an opinion." Write the three purposes on the board and explain each, using one of the books as a visual and to provide concrete examples.

2. **Group Activity**: Organize students into six groups, and give each group one of the model books. Ask each group to examine its book and complete section 1 of the handout. Then have each group present its findings to the class. **Note**: Each group's members and model book should remain the same throughout the rest of this lesson.

3. **Full-Class Discussion** (next class period): Explain the concept of a text's audience. You might say, "Every text has not only a purpose but a target *audience* too. The audience is the type of reader that the author had in mind when he or she wrote the book. For example, the target audience might be a certain age. The target audience might be male or female or might be a student or a parent or a teacher. The target audience might be teenagers who want to know about the solar system or fourth graders who want to be entertained by a story about a boy who has magic powers. An author chooses what to say based on who is listening—who the target audience is."

4. **Group Activity**: Have students break into their groups. Ask each group to examine its book and complete section 2 of the handout. Then have each group share its findings with the class.

5. **Full-Class Discussion** (next class period): Explain the concept of a writer's tasks. To develop this part of the lesson, you can refer to the tasks listed in the Common

Core Writing Standards 1 to 3 for grades 4 and 5. To limit the scope of this lesson, you might choose to focus on the task of organizing information. You might say, "Once an author decides the text's purpose and audience, he or she has to carry out the *tasks* of writing. The tasks are different, depending on the purpose for writing. For example, to tell a story, the author might arrange events in the order in which they happened. The author of a biography might do the same thing. To explain an opinion, the author might state the opinion and then give reasons to support the opinion."

6. **Group Activity**: Have students assemble in their groups. Ask each group to examine its book and complete section 3 of the handout. Then have each group share its findings with the class.

7. **Wrap-Up**: For homework, have students work independently to write explanatory essays. Students should

   - Write for an audience of their classmates. This means they should briefly explain new terms and mention how this information is useful to a fourth or fifth grader (the latter task would help make a great conclusion).
   - Give the title and author's name of the book they are writing about.
   - Use their completed handout as a resource to explain the purpose of, audience for, and organization of the book.
   - Include at least five paragraphs: an introduction, a paragraph on purpose, a paragraph on audience, a paragraph on organization, and a concluding statement or paragraph.
   - Check their work for complete sentences, capitalization, punctuation, and spelling.

Extend the Lesson

- Have students bring in examples of their writing for school and writing they have done outside school (stories or blogs, for example). Ask students to write or present orally explanations of the purpose, audience, and method of organization of their texts.

- Schedule class time to conference with students one-on-one or in groups as they write their essays. Consider scheduling one in-class writing session.

Differentiation

For students who need extra support
- Have students complete the writing assignment as a shared writing task. Guide them to divide the writing tasks among group members. For example, each student can work with a partner to write one paragraph of the total piece.

For advanced students
- For the writing assignment, allow students to choose a text from a list of choices to use as the subject of their writing.

Assessment

Use this rubric to evaluate students' essays.

	Purpose	Audience	Tasks	Language
Score: 4	Essay is informative or explanatory.	Audience is classmates.	Names title and author of book. Introduces topic. Explains purpose. Explains audience. Explains organization. Has conclusion.	Makes no major errors in conventions.
Score: 3	Essay is informative or explanatory.	Audience is classmates or a teacher.	Achieves the tasks listed in Score 4 but includes some irrelevant or erroneous information.	Makes a few noticeable errors in conventions.
Score: 2	Essay is mainly informative or explanatory but goes off target to narrate or summarize part of the text.	Audience is a general reader.	Achieves several of the tasks listed in Score 4. May include irrelevant or erroneous information.	Makes numerous errors in conventions.
Score: 1	A paragraph or two is informative, but most of essay retells the text or gives opinions.	No clear audience.	Achieves one or two tasks listed in Score 4.	Errors in conventions make reading or understanding the essay difficult.
Score: 0	Essay retells the text or gives opinions.	No clear audience.	Achieves none of the tasks listed in Score 4.	Errors in conventions make the essay unreadable or unintelligible.

Additional Resources

SlideShare has a tutorial called "Teaching Text Structure: A Quick Guide for Teachers" that you can use to extend this lesson or to create writing assignments targeted to specific text structures: slideshare.net/elkissn/teaching-text-structure.

Notes

After implementing the lesson, make notes on what worked and what you would change next time.

_____

_____

_____

_____

Purpose, Audience, and Task Activity Sheet

Use the book your teacher provided to answer the following questions. Use the notes space to record helpful ideas from the book, your group members, or your teacher.

Section 1: Purpose

	Notes
1. What is the book's main purpose: to tell a story, to give information, or to explain an opinion?	
2. What details or examples in the book help you figure out the book's purpose?	

Section 2: Audience

	Notes
3. How would you describe the book's target audience?	
4. What details or examples in the book help you know who its audience is?	

Section 3: Writer's Task

	Notes
5. How does the author arrange information or events in the book?	
6. What details or examples in the book helped you identify how the author arranged information?	

Let's Blog!

Use a Classroom Blog Site

Grade Levels: 4–5

Time Frame: Approximately two class periods

Overview: This lesson guides students through the process of writing a blog entry, commenting on others' blog entries, and replying to comments. Although the lesson requires students to follow standard conventions of writing, it opens up the possibilities of topic, audience, and purpose. Blogging can be fun! Once a classroom blog site is established, students can return to it throughout the school year as a medium for writing assignments of all sorts.

Common Core State Standards
- 4: Writing, Standard 6: With some guidance and support from adults, use technology, including the Internet, to produce and publish writing as well as to interact and collaborate with others; demonstrate sufficient command of keyboarding skills to type a minimum of one page in a single sitting.

- 5: Writing, Standard 6: With some guidance and support from adults, use technology, including the Internet, to produce and publish writing as well as to interact and collaborate with others; demonstrate sufficient command of keyboarding skills to type a minimum of two pages in a single sitting.

- 4–5: Writing, Standard 10: Write routinely over extended time frames (time for research, reflection, and revision) and shorter time frames (a single sitting or a day or two) for a range of discipline-specific tasks, purposes, and audiences.

Objectives
- Students will use a blog as a digital medium for producing and publishing their writing.

Background Knowledge Required
No particular background knowledge is required for this lesson.

Materials Needed
- Set up a teacher-moderated blogging platform for your class. A suggested free site is Kidblog.org. Teachers designed it for teachers, and protection for the safety of student bloggers is built in.

- A few kid-friendly blog entries to read aloud as models and inspiration. Here are a few suggestions:

  - Any of the science-themed blogs on Steve Spangler Science: www.stevespangler.com
  - Any of the kid-written book review blogs on DogEared: kidsblogs .nationalgeographic.com/dogeared
  - "6 Things Kids Must Remember When Blogging": www.kidslearntoblog.com/ 6-things-kids-must-remember-when-blogging

Agenda

1. **Introduction**: Begin by reading a short blog or part of a longer blog, chosen specifically to win students' interest or attention. Go on to explain what a blog is by telling how it compares and contrasts to familiar media such as diaries, letters, magazine articles, school reports, Tweets, texts, and so on. Point out that a regular blog usually follows a theme, such as science, fashion, sports, books, movies, family, friends, or something else. The possibilities are practically endless! Ask if anyone has ever published a blog post online and, if so, what his or her experience was like. Tell students that soon, all of them will be bloggers.

2. **Blogging Activity**: Depending on the availability of computers with Internet access, have students work all at once or organize them into groups that can work one at a time. Have each student access the classroom blog platform, log in, and type in a blog entry. Specify a theme for the blogs, and give basic guidelines for what you expect. For example, a blog can be one or more paragraphs long, and it must focus on a single topic or question. This is not a text message, a Tweet, or a phone message, so the blog must follow the conventions of spelling, capitalization, and punctuation. For a great list of suggested themes and topics, read Pernille Ripp's "Student Blogging Challenges: A List of Ideas," posted here: pernilleripp.com/2012/04/student -blogging-challenges-list-of.html. A couple of the categories are All about School (e.g., "What would you change about school so that you would love being there?") and Wacky Challenges (e.g., "How many ways can you use a paperclip?").

3. **Commenting Activity** (next class period): Have students read three (or a number you decide) of their classmates' blogs and post a thoughtful comment to each. Explain that a *thoughtful* comment has *thought* behind it. For example, it offers positive feedback on an idea the blogger expressed well, it asks a question related to one of the blogger's ideas, it connects one of the blogger's ideas to an idea of the commenter's own, or it recommends a related blog and tells why. To ensure that every blogger receives at least one comment, you might assign one "must read" to each student and then let him or her choose an additional blog or two to read.

   Also have students write thoughtful replies to comments their blogs receive. A thoughtful reply shows appreciation for a comment by pointing out how it was interesting or helpful. If the commenter asked a question, a thoughtful reply answers the question without making the commenter feel silly for asking.

4. **Wrap-Up**: Have a class discussion about how blogs can be educational, entertaining, and fun to follow. Have students generate a shared list of goals for upcoming entries in their new blog. Ideas might include writing one entry per week, sharing opinions

about reading assignments, sharing the results of science experiments, reporting on a school club or activity, switching to a different blog theme and then sticking to it, and so on.

Differentiation

For students who need extra support

- Pair up students who are intimidated by technology with students who are confident with technology. Or form work groups that include at least one technology leader, one strong writer, and one social leader.

For advanced students

- Allow students to add appropriate graphics, sound effects, and sound clips to their blogs. Have them show the class how they did it.

Assessment

Have students write blog entries that report on what they have learned about blogging so far, what questions they still have, and what their number-one goals are as bloggers. Remind students to follow conventions of spelling, capitalization, and punctuation but encourage them to have fun with their tone and style (i.e., use humor, use sports analogies, etc.). Use the blogs to assess whether additional technical instruction is needed or whether students are ready to tackle new blogging assignments.

Additional Resources

For more blogging ideas and information, go to Kids Learn to Blog: www.kidslearntoblog.com. One of the articles, "Express Yourself with Blogging," reviews several high-interest blogs written by kids:www.kidslearntoblog.com/express-yourself-with-blogging

Notes

After implementing the lesson, make notes on what worked and what you would change next time.

_____

_____

_____

_____

In a Nutshell

Summarize Information

Grade Level: 5

Time Frame: Approximately two class periods

Overview: This lesson introduces the task of summarizing. It has students explore the word itself and brainstorm for the specifics of what a summary is and what it isn't. Students work with partners to write and revise a summary of a short text. In the Common Core, fifth grade is the only grade to focus on summarizing as a distinct writing task. Beginning in sixth grade, the standards have students provide summaries as a reading task, with both literature and informational texts.

Common Core State Standards
- 5: Writing, Standard 4: Produce clear and coherent writing in which the development, organization, and style are appropriate to task, purpose, and audience.

- 5: Writing, Standard 6: With some guidance and support from adults, use technology, including the Internet, to produce and publish writing as well as to interact and collaborate with others.

- 5: Writing, Standard 8: Recall relevant information from experience or gather relevant information from print and digital sources; summarize or paraphrase information in notes and finished work, and provide a list of sources.

- 5: Writing, Standard 10: Write routinely over extended time frames (time for research, reflection, and revision) and shorter time frames (a single sitting or a day or two) for a range of discipline-specific tasks, purposes, and audiences.

Objectives
- Students will learn what a summary is and reasons writers write them.

- In a shared writing activity, students will write and revise a summary of a nonfiction text.

Background Knowledge Required
- Use this lesson in conjunction with a short nonfiction text students have read for class, such as a magazine article or section of a textbook chapter.

- Students should be familiar with the terms *main topic, main idea,* and *opinion.*

Materials Needed

- Copies of a nonfiction text that students have read

- Copies of the handout: Summary Activity Sheet, p. 120

Agenda

1. **Introduction**: Tell students that an important skill for any writer is the ability to write a summary of a text. Hold up a book or other printed text, and introduce it. Then read aloud a short summary of the text. You could read a summary from the book jacket or write your own.

2. **Full-Class Activity**: Pass out copies of the handout. Have students use their existing knowledge to help you fill in information in all sections of the graphic organizer except the example summary. When necessary, guide students to discover information (e.g., ask volunteers to look up a definition and additional word forms in a dictionary). As students deplete their own knowledge, teach to fill in the gaps. For example, a summary is shorter than the original text, is objective, tells the title and author of the text it summarizes, gives the main topic and main ideas of the text, and does not copy the text's exact words. A summary is *not* (or does not contain) opinions, critiques or commentary on the text, reviews or other judgments of the text, comparisons to other texts, or a detailed paraphrase of the entire text. Writers use summaries as *parts of* book reviews, research papers, opinion texts, blogs, podcasts, and other written or spoken texts that share information and sometimes build upon or argue with that information.

3. **Partner Activity**: Have students work with partners to write summaries. First, have them reread the informational text that you chose to use. Direct them to mark up the page or take notes to identify the text's main idea and important points. Have them write drafts of their summaries on separate paper.

4. **Peer Feedback Activity** (next class period): As a class, create a summary feedback checklist to guide the revision process. Use the graphic organizer's sections on "What it is" and "What it's not" to inspire the checklist, writing it on the board for reference. Then have each pair of students work with another pair of students to give feedback on the drafts of their summaries.

5. **Wrap-Up**: Have students write their revised summaries in the graphic organizers.

Extend the Lesson

- Have students practice summarizing the text in different lengths for different purposes. Scaffold from a Tweet to a text to a social networking post (e.g., Facebook) and then to the blog entry described in the following bullet.

- Have students write blog entries in which they review a book or short story. The review should begin with an objective summary of the text before moving on to giving opinions about it. Have students read and write comments on at least one classmate's blog entry.

Differentiation

For students who need extra support

- Have students identify main ideas and details of individual paragraphs and then summarize those paragraphs before you have them go on to summarize a longer text.

For advanced students

- Have students incorporate one direct quotation (of a phrase or sentence) into their summaries.

Assessment

- Use the student-generated summary feedback checklist to evaluate the shared-writing summaries. For example, award points to the final drafts based on how many items in the checklist are completed successfully. Or use the checklist to describe a top-score response (say, on a 4-point scale).

- Once you score the summaries, allow students the opportunity to revise their summaries for a higher score. Students could work on the revisions independently or with their original partners.

Additional Resources

TV 411 has an interactive lesson that helps students practice individual tasks that contribute to writing a strong summary: www.tv411.org/reading/understanding-what-you -read/summarizing. Even if you don't have students go online to do the activities, you can use the activities to inspire your own lesson extensions.

Notes

After implementing the lesson, make notes on what worked and what you would change the next time.

_____

_____

_____

_____

Summary Activity Sheet

Summary	
Part of speech: Definition:	Other word forms:
What it is:	What it's not:
Where writers use summaries:	
Example of a summary:	

Speaking and Listening

Part 3

Overview

To teach the Common Core State Standards for Speaking and Listening, think in terms of variety. Students need to learn to speak in front of different sized audiences on a range of different topics. Give students "ample opportunities to take part in a variety of rich, structured conversations—as part of a whole class, in small groups, and with a partner" (Common Core State Standards, p. 22). For example, your speaking lessons can include small-group discussions about a text students are reading, partner discussions about students' topics for opinion-based essays, and oral presentations in front of the full class. Teach students speaking skills such as maintaining eye contact, assuming a confident posture, and speaking clearly and at a reasonable pace. Also teach students how to listen to others and how to agree or disagree respectfully. For more suggestions for revising your lessons or creating new lessons, see the checklist below.

Planning Checklist

When planning a CCSS-based speaking and listening lesson, keep the following tips in mind.

☐ Plan academic discussions around literature and informational texts that students are reading in class. Require students to refer to the text when they answer questions about it. For example, if you're having a class discussion about *Curious George* and a student makes a comment about the monkey causing trouble, ask that student what part of the story made him or her think that.

☐ At times, give students the opportunity to prepare in advance for a discussion. This is particularly helpful for shy students, who might not be comfortable forming or saying their opinions on the spot. For example, they can write down one idea or one sentence they'll want to share in the discussion.

☐ Model good speaking and listening behaviors for students. For example, you can play "show me listening." You model what listening to someone looks like—make eye contact, nod, ask a relevant question, etc.—and then ask students to do the same (Roberts and Billings, 2012, p. 22). You can give students simple checklists or goals sheets to assess themselves before or after a discussion.

☐ Teach students that disagreeing is OK. However, they need to do so respectfully. You may wish to give students sentence frames to show them ways to disagree. For example, "Caylee has a good point, but I think X." You may want to create discussion rules as a class, rather than just giving students the rules. Doing so will help students think critically about appropriate behavior and make them more inclined to follow the rules because they helped make them themselves.

☐ Show students how to deliver information to an audience using an audio or a visual aid. That aid can be as simple as a poster or something higher-level, such as a PowerPoint presentation, depending on students' ages and experience. Discuss that such an aid enhances an audience's understanding of a topic but must be used carefully so it doesn't distract the audience.

☐ When a student is delivering a presentation, you can have the other students show they're listening and require each person to write down one question about the presentation or summarize the presentation so they can practice their listening skills and are not just waiting for their turns.

☐ Create rubrics along with students for assessing speaking and listening skills.

☐ When teaching literature and informational texts, you can have students listen to an audio or watch a video version or listen to classmates read parts aloud. You can also consider using digital texts, which "confront students with the potential for continually updated content and dynamically changing combinations of words, graphics, images, hyperlinks, and embedded video and audio" (The Common Core State Standards, p. 22). Some sources of interactive e-books are available here: www.ehow.com/list_7480757 _interactive-ebooks-children.html. Students can create their own digital storybooks, too—some examples can be found online by googling *digital storybooks* or *digital storytelling* and *elementary school.*

Lesson Plans at a Glance

Five Senses

Describe People, Places, Things, or Events

Grade Levels: K–1; adaptable to grades 2–5 (see note in Overview)

Time Frame: Approximately one class period

Overview: Students in grades K–5 are asked to describe people, places, things, or events when speaking and listening to others. In kindergarten and first grade, the emphasis is on providing details along with support drawings or visual displays to provide additional details. In addition, students are expected to speak audibly and express their thoughts, feelings, and ideas clearly for others to understand. Although this lesson is designed for kindergarten and first grade, you can adapt it to higher grades by requiring students to speak and write their descriptions. Students can work on using more descriptive adjectives in their descriptions or tying them more closely to a past memory.

Common Core State Standards
- K: Speaking and Listening, Standard 4: Describe familiar people, places, things, and events and, with prompting and support, provide additional detail.

- 1: Speaking and Listening, Standard 4: Describe people, places, things, and events with relevant details, expressing ideas and feelings clearly.

- K: Speaking and Listening, Standard 5: Add drawings or other visual displays to descriptions as desired to provide additional detail.

- 1: Speaking and Listening, Standard 5: Add drawings or other visual displays to descriptions when appropriate to clarify ideas, thoughts, and feelings.

- K: Speaking and Listening, Standard 6: Speak audibly and express thoughts, feelings, and ideas clearly.

Objectives
- Students will use clear, specific words to describe people, places, things, or events to others.

- Students will create drawings that, when used with oral descriptions, describe people, places, things, or event to others.

Background Knowledge Required
Students should know and understand their five senses.

Materials Needed

- Paper and drawing implements for students

- Pictures of people, places, things, or events (optional)

- Copies of the handout: Writing Descriptions Based on the Five Senses (optional), p. 128

Agenda

1. **Introduction**: Tell students that people use words to paint pictures of people, places, things, or events they enjoy. Today they will use the five senses to describe things they know about. Their senses help people describe things to paint pictures for others and help them express how they feel. Discuss each of the senses with students.

   Next, choose one topic to explore, and then help students create a short list of people, places, things, or events that students know about. For example, as a group you may create a list of foods students like to eat. On the board, narrow the list to one or two items to describe using the senses.

2. **Modeling Activity**: Now that you have one or two items students know about and are able to describe, walk them through one description. To model creating a description, write the words or picture clues for the five senses, such as a hand, a mouth, an eye, an ear, and a nose. Use them as a checklist to model how students can create descriptions or paint pictures with their words. Or pass out the optional student handout for students to use as checklists. For example, ask students to think about an apple. How does an apple feel in the hands? How does an apple taste? What does an apple look like? How does an apple sound when a person bites into it? How does an apple smell? Based on the item chosen to describe, teach students words that are appropriate for their descriptions, such as *heavy, light, sour, sweet, tangy, smooth, shiny, red, yellow, green, crunchy*, etc. Next ask students to make connections to the item described, such as an apple. Why do they like or not like to eat apples?

3. **Full-Class Activity**: As a class, choose something to describe from the list. Ask students to use their five senses as a checklist to describe the item. Guide students to be specific and use appropriate descriptive words. Help students make personal connections to the item they are describing. Again, students could use the handout to write their describing words as the class creates the list.

4. **Independent Activity**: Pass out a piece of paper and coloring implements to each student. Tell students it is their turn to use their descriptive words as guides to help them draw the item the class just described. Remind students to be specific in their drawings; they should show the shiny skin or color of the apple, the texture of the inside, etc. For kindergarten students, add a tactile element to the picture. If you are working with an apple, choose buttons or beans for students to glue on to the pictures of the cut apple. Use this opportunity to talk about the texture of the "seeds."

5. **Wrap-Up**: Have students pair up and describe their pictures to their partners.

Extend the Lesson

Tell students that today they will play a guessing game; they will have to guess what is being described from the list. Choose one of the people, places, or events from the list and begin describing it for the students without telling them specifics. For example, if describing the beach, you might say something such as, "This place has lots of sand. The water meets the sand with crashing waves. It is a fun place to build sandcastles. Your family may visit this place in the summer. Where am I?" Encourage students to be specific in their descriptions. Point out the descriptions you used to describe the item from your list.

Differentiation

For students who need extra support

- Use pictures in a pocket chart of people, places, or events. Have students choose one and describe what they see in the picture. Ask students to tell you the colors they see, a story they are reminded of, or how they feel about the picture.

- For the independent activity, have students use pictures from a magazine or stamps to create their pictures if they are not comfortable drawing.

- Have all students use the same picture, such as a picture from a book, a magazine, or an old calendar, and take turns describing it without having to come up with the image on their own.

For advanced students

- During the full-class activity, ask volunteers to write words in the chart for you.

- During the independent activity, have students write out a sentence or two describing their pictures without stating who or what is in the picture.

- During the modeling activity, brainstorm a list of describing words for each category for students to refer to or use when creating their descriptions. Examples for people would be *young, old, tall, short, wearing a colored shirt*, etc.

Assessment

- Check that students created appropriate pictures in the independent activity. Do the pictures match the item described? Are the colors correct? Do the pictures show detail? Do the pictures show the students' personal connections?

- To check for students' understanding of the describing words, show students two similar pictures and describe one of them. Have students identify the correct picture, such as a picture of a boy at the beach in a blue bathing suit vs. a picture of a girl at the park in a blue bathing suit.

- For the extension activity, place two pictures in a pocket chart. Organize students into pairs. To check for their understanding of descriptions, ask one student to describe one of the pictures and the other to guess which picture is being described.

Additional Resources

- Show students magazine photographs, old calendar pictures, or pictures from books, and ask them to describe what they see.

- Older students could use the handout to write their lists of descriptors.

Notes

After implementing the lesson, make notes on what worked and what you would change next time.

_____

_____

_____

_____

Writing Descriptions Based on the Five Senses

Complete the chart to describe something using your five senses.

Person, Place, Thing, or Event I'm Describing: _____

Sense	Description
✋	
👂	
👃	
👄	
👁	

Talk, Talk, Talk

Participate in Collaborative Discussions

Grade Levels: K–1

Time Frame: Approximately one class period

Overview: Students in grades K–5 are asked to participate in collaborative discussions with diverse partners about grade-level specific topics and texts with peers and adults in small and larger groups. Teaching students in the early grades about appropriate discussion behavior and ways to participate in discussions will give students a lifelong skill they can use in the future.

Common Core State Standards

- K: Speaking and Listening, Standard 1: Participate in collaborative conversations with diverse partners about *kindergarten topics and texts* with peers and adults in small and larger groups. a. Follow agreed-upon rules for discussions (e.g., listening to others and taking turns speaking about the topics and texts under discussion). b. Continue a conversation through multiple exchanges.

- K: Speaking and Listening, Standard 2: Confirm understanding of a text read aloud or information presented orally or through other media by asking and answering questions about key details and requesting clarification if something is not understood.

- 1: Speaking and Listening, Standard 1: Participate in collaborative conversations with diverse partners about *grade 1 topics and texts* with peers and adults in small and larger groups. a. Follow agreed-upon rules for discussions (e.g., listening to others with care, speaking one at a time about the topics and texts under discussion). b. Build on others' talk in conversations by responding to the comments of others through multiple exchanges. c. Ask questions to clear up any confusion about the topics and texts under discussion.

- 1: Speaking and Listening, Standard 2: Ask and answer questions about key details in a text read aloud or information presented orally or through other media.

Objectives

- Students will participate in a collaborative discussion with peers about a grade-level text.

- Students will listen appropriately, share opinions, and (when appropriate) ask questions for clarification.

Background Knowledge Required

Students must understand taking turns when participating in discussions.

Materials Needed

- Grade-level text in big book format, such as *Sylvester and the Magic Pebble*, by William Steig

- Copies of the handout: I Have Something to Say!, p. 133

Agenda

1. **Introduction**: Tell students that you are going to read a story to them today. They need to listen to this story, even if it is a familiar one, because after the reading, the class is going to discuss it. Tell students, "During a discussion, different people share their thoughts or information about a particular topic or text. Before I read the story, we should review discussion rules." These rules should be already in place in your classroom. Some sample discussion rules might be

   - Listen carefully to what others say.
   - Ask questions if you need more information.
   - Wait your turn to talk. Raise your hand to share and be patient.

   You might wish to involve students in creating the rules; they might feel more responsibility to stick with them. Ask students why each rule is important.

   Read the chosen story aloud. Give students the handout so they can jot down a question or comment that comes to mind during the reading. Tell them that they will share a question or comment during the discussion right after they listen to the story.

2. **Full-Class Activity**: Tell students it is time to discuss the book. Begin by asking students about the main characters and the setting. Guide students through the discussion by asking questions, encouraging students to participate, asking students to clarify answers, and making sure students take turns and listen to one another. Have students share the questions that they wrote on their handouts. Point out how students are interacting during the discussion. For example, say, "Good job taking turns and waiting for someone else to talk."

   Here are some questions for the discussion of *Sylvester and the Magic Pebble*. If you chose a different story, alter these questions or create your own for the discussion.

   - Who is the main character?
   - Where does the story take place?
   - What is Sylvester's personality like?
   - Does Sylvester do mainly good things or bad things in this story? Give some examples.
   - What do you like most about Sylvester? Why?
   - What do you like least about Sylvester? Why?

   ### Discussion Hints

   If students struggle with taking turns, you may want to pass out an item for students to hold when it is their turn to talk. This item could be a ball, a small rain stick, or even a special pencil. Students may share only when they are holding the "talking item." When a student has spoken, he or she passes the item to the next student. Students who are not holding the "talking item" should listen to the speaker.

If a student is shy about sharing, ask specific questions that do not have right or wrong answers, such as "What was your favorite part of the story?" Remind students that people's opinions are not right or wrong. It is all right to feel differently from one another, but people should respect one another's thoughts by listening to other people speak. You might even want to model listening to another person during a discussion. For example, people make eye contact rather than doodling or doing their own work. They also show that they're listening by acknowledging what a person who spoke previously said before giving their own thoughts. Give students sentence starters such as, "I agree with _____ because _____" or "_____ [student's name] had an interesting opinion, but I think that _____ ."

If this particular book did not spark an interest in one or more students, try relating the questions or book back to another book students read or listened to together. Can students make comparisons between the two stories?

3. **Wrap-Up**: Tell students that now that they know how to have a discussion about a text and can take turns listening, asking questions, and telling opinions, they will be able to participate in future discussions with peers and adults alike.

Extend the Lesson

Tell students they are going to take a text home to read aloud with parents. Choose a text, and include open-ended discussion questions for parents and students. Encourage students to practice listening, asking questions, and telling opinions. Once students master how to have a book discussion, you can use the technique throughout the year as part of the regular English language arts curriculum.

Differentiation

For students who need extra support

- Use a simpler text, and do the full-class activity in small groups so that students do not have to wait as long to participate.

- Have students listen to a text on tape and participate in small-group discussions that you or another adult monitor.

For advanced students

- Change the text for these students.

- Ask these students to come up with their own questions for the discussion. Allow the discussion to be student run instead of teacher run.

Assessment

Give students a checklist of what you are looking for in a discussion, such as listening, asking questions, and sharing opinions. Use this rubric as students participate. Are they listening? Are they asking appropriate questions? Are they sharing opinions? The rubric should be grade appropriate. For kindergarten students, a smiley face rubric may be best. For first-grade students, a number rubric or smiley face rubric may work. Here is a sample rubric.

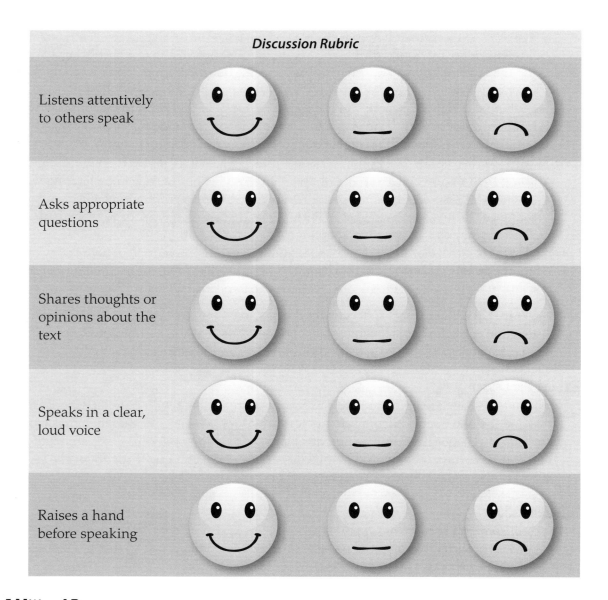

Discussion Rubric

Additional Resources

- A number of free websites have sample rubrics or rubric builders for teachers to use to create their own rubrics. www.rubrics4teachers.com is an example of one site.

Notes

After implementing the lesson, make notes on what worked and what you would change next time.

_____

_____

_____

_____

I Have Something to Say!

Think of a question or comment about the story to share with the class. Write it in the box below. You can also draw a picture of it if you want.

Do You Hear What I Hear?

Listen to Others Speak

Grade Levels: 2–3

Time Frame: Approximately one class period

Overview: Elementary school students are asked to ask and answer questions about what a speaker says in order to clarify comprehension. In K–1, the focus is on gathering information. In grades 2–3, the emphasis is on deepening understanding of a topic or an issue. In addition, students are expected to report on a topic, tell a story, or recount an experience using appropriate facts and details. They are also expected to speak audibly and at an understandable pace.

Common Core State Standards

- 2: Speaking and Listening, Standard 3: Ask and answer questions about what a speaker says in order to clarify comprehension, gather additional information, or deepen understanding of a topic or an issue.

- 3: Speaking and Listening, Standard 3: Ask and answer questions about information from a speaker, offering appropriate elaboration and detail.

Objectives

- Students will learn to ask questions of a speaker to clarify understanding.

- Students will speak clearly, audibly, and at an understandable pace.

Background Knowledge Required

No special background knowledge is required for this lesson.

Materials Needed

- Pictures from old magazines, newspapers, books, or calendars that can be used to tell a story

- Recorded short story and audio player

Agenda

1. **Introduction**: Tell students that today they are going to play the parts of reporters! A good reporter always asks questions to find additional information and details in order to clarify understanding. Questions usually start with one of these question words: *who, what, where, when, why,* and *how.* Write these words on the board as a

reference for students. A *who* question helps clarify the people in the story. A *what* question helps determine the plot of the story or presentation and can help clarify the details. A *where* question can clarify the location of the story. A *when* question helps the listener identify the timing of events of the story. A *why* question can clarify the reason an event happens in a story. Finally, a *how* question provides details of the events in the story.

2. **Modeling Activity**: Model creating questions while listening to a short story on tape. Play the short story, and pause to point out a good place to ask a question. Have students practice asking appropriate questions, and then continue listening to the story.

3. **Full-Class Activity**: Choose a topic to tell students about. This may be a current event, a social studies or science topic, or something else relevant to what students are learning in your class. Tell students that you will share information about the topic with them, and they will need to be reporters, listening to what you say and creating questions to clarify any information that is confusing or needs more explanation. As you tell your story/share your topic, pause for questions as appropriate. Remind students to use the questioning words to clarify their understanding of what you are sharing. Answer the questions as you continue telling the story/sharing the topic. Also point out the pace at which you're asking the questions. Tell students they need to speak clearly so other people can understand their question.

4. **Wrap-Up**: Ask students who, what, where, when, why, and how questions about the shared topic that will help clarify their understanding. Have students practice answering the questions aloud.

Extend the Lesson

Have students write their own who, what, where, when, why and how questions based on the shared topic. These questions may be simple in nature or more complex depending on students' writing abilities. After students write their questions, meet as a whole class, and have students practice asking and answering one another's questions. Remind students to speak clearly and purposefully when they ask their questions.

Differentiation

For students who need extra support
- Do the full-class activity in guided group settings in which you can guide the process a little more closely.

For advanced students
- Have advanced students write formal reports based on their findings from the shared topic and the questions asked and answered. Students can share their reporting with the class.

- Ask students to create their own stories not based on pictures you provide.

- Have students listen to another story/topic on tape. Have students write appropriate questions that help clarify their understanding of the story. Remind students to use appropriate questioning words.

Assessment

Choose a new topic, and have each student ask an appropriate question that will clarify understanding about the topic. Students can do this orally or on paper. Check that students use an appropriate questioning word (*who, what, where, when, why,* or *how*).

Additional Resources

- *The Kids' Book of Questions,* by Gregory Stock, provides questions that students can answer, allowing them to practice their questioning skills. From those questions, teach students to ask follow-up questions of their classmates.

Notes

After implementing the lesson, make notes on what worked and what you would change next time.

_____

_____

_____

_____

Testing, Testing, 1, 2, 3 . . .

Create Audio Recordings

Grade Levels: 2–3

Time Frame: Approximately one class period

Overview: Students in grades 2–3 create audio recordings of stories and poems that demonstrate reading with appropriate pace and fluidity. This lesson will give students practice with those skills.

Common Core State Standards

- 2: Speaking and Listening, Standard 5: Create audio recordings of stories or poems; add drawings or other visual displays to stories or recounts of experiences when appropriate to clarify ideas, thoughts, and feelings.

- 3: Speaking and Listening, Standard 5: Create engaging audio recordings of stories or poems that demonstrate fluid reading at an understandable pace; add visual displays when appropriate to emphasize or enhance certain facts or details.

- 2: Reading, Foundational Skills, Standard 4: Read with sufficient accuracy and fluency to support comprehension. a. Read on-level text with purpose and understanding. b. Read on-level text orally with accuracy, appropriate rate, and expression on successive readings. c. Use context to confirm or self-correct word recognition and understanding, rereading as necessary.

- 3: Reading, Foundational Skills, Standard 4: Read with sufficient accuracy and fluency to support comprehension. a. Read on-level text with purpose and understanding. b. Read on-level prose and poetry orally with accuracy, appropriate rate, and expression on successive readings. c. Use context to confirm or self-correct word recognition and understanding, rereading as necessary.

Objectives

- Students will practice correcting themselves and adjusting their pace while reading a poem or short story aloud.

Background Knowledge Required

No particular background knowledge is required for this lesson.

Materials Needed
- Recording device (computer with microphone and recording capabilities, tape recorder, etc.)

- Two short stories or poems at the students' reading levels

Agenda
1. **Introduction**: Children have been reciting poetry and short stories for years and years! Tell students that reciting poems and short stories not only builds speaking skills but also builds numerous language arts skills. Repeated readings of a text build fluency for students. Adding an element of performance provides context for reading a passage over and over. When students perform, they also must take the time to really understand what they have read so they can read expressively. Tell students that they will practice reading a chosen poem or short story with appropriate pace and expression.

2. **Modeling Activity**: Model for students how to read a short story or poem using appropriate pacing. First, read a portion to students at a quick pace. Ask students if that pace sounded right, and have them describe why it did or did not. Then read another portion, this time with no expression. Ask students if they want you to keep reading that way. They should respond that it sounds boring and that the reading has no meaning when there is no expression. Tell students it is their turn to practice reading.

3. **Full-Class Activity**: Pass out copies of one of the short stories or poems. Choose one sentence, and have students read it aloud together as quickly as they can. Did it sound appropriate? Now, have them read the same line, this time concentrating on their pacing. Discuss how pacing adds meaning to a text and that students need to practice pacing to aid comprehension.

    Next, have students read a line with no expression. Ask, "How does hearing that part of the poem or story without any expression make you feel?" Discuss the point of expression. Then ask students to read another line, this time with expression. By this point, students should have an understanding of pace and expression.

4. **Partner Activity**: Pair students up and pass out another short story or poem. Have students and their partners practice reading their short stories or poems with expression and appropriate pacing. Once students are ready, they may record their pieces, using the device of choice in the classroom. (See additional resources for online recording tools.)

5. **Wrap-Up**: Choose a few students to share their recordings of their short stories or poems. Over the next few days, you could share all the students' recordings.

Extend the Lesson
Students could write their own short stories or poems and record themselves reading them aloud. If you choose to use online recording tools, students could also create and upload pictures to match their short stories or poems.

To address the second part of standard 5, have students create visuals to accompany their audio recordings. Visuals could include the students' own drawings or cut-out/printed pictures.

Differentiation

For students who need extra support
- Have two students record a short story or poem together.

For advanced students
- Have advanced students use different voices to read short stories or poems that have multiple characters. Record the stories or poems.

Assessment

Listen to students' recordings. Check for appropriate pacing and expression when they speak. Work with students who did not read at the appropriate pace or use appropriate expression to enhance their fluency before having them record again.

Additional Resources

- A number of online recording tools and websites are safe for students to use. Many also allow uploading a photo to match a recording and are shared only with students in the class or with other students around the country or world. Some to check out include Animoto, Stupeflix, SourceForge, Wavosaur, Mediafire, Flixtime, and Fotobabble.

Notes

After implementing the lesson, make notes on what worked and what you would change next time.

_____

_____

_____

_____

Do You Hear What I Hear?

Learning to Paraphrase

Grade Level: 4

Time Frame: Approximately one class period

Overview: Students in grades K–5 respond to a text read aloud. In fourth grade, appropriate student responses include paraphrasing portions of a text that are presented orally or through a variety of multimedia formats. This lesson will show students how to paraphrase effectively.

Common Core State Standards

- 4: Speaking and Listening, Standard 2: Paraphrase portions of a text read aloud or information presented in diverse media and formats, including visually, quantitatively, and orally.

Objectives

- Students will listen closely to information shared orally.

- Students will paraphrase information thoroughly and accurately.

Background Knowledge Required

Students should have knowledge of synonyms.

Materials Needed

- Grade-level text for students to paraphrase

Agenda

1. **Introduction**: Introduce paraphrasing to students. Explain that paraphrasing is restating a text or passage to give the information in another way. Students think about the text and then put it into their own words. When students paraphrase something they hear, they communicate the gist of the message without repeating everything word for word. Learning to paraphrase is a great tool for comprehending information because putting information into their own words helps ensure students' understanding. Point out the difference between paraphrasing and plagiarizing. When you paraphrase, you put it into your own words and it helps you understand the information, or it helps you explain the information to other people. If you plagiarize, you are stealing someone else's words.

Give students a concrete example of paraphrasing. Begin by explaining that before students try a new sport, they might want to read about it. For example, they might want to know how to play and if you need any special equipment. Read students a simple informational text, such as this description of soccer. http://kids .discovery.com/tell-me/curiosity-corner/sports/how-to-play-soccer

Tell students it is time to think about these statements and put them in their own words. Paraphrasing the text will help them comprehend it. And maybe it will help them explain soccer to one of their friends. You might say something such as, "Soccer is a game played by two teams where each team tries to kick the ball into the other team's net. Your team wins if it gets the most goals. Each team has a goalie, who stands in the net and tries to stop the goals. You don't need a lot of equipment to play soccer, but goalies need more padding so they don't get hurt by the ball." Now let's check and see if I got the gist of the information." Compare the original to your paraphrase. Point out that you got the main bits of information but did not repeat it word for word.

2. **Modeling Activity**: Tell students that today they will practice paraphrasing. Write these sample sentences on the board, or create your own sentences for students to paraphrase. As a class, walk through how to paraphrase these sentences by replacing words with synonyms, reworking sentence structures, and putting the ideas into your own words. A paraphrase is more than just changing a word here and there.

> To be a pilot, you first have to go to commercial pilot ground school. You have to fly at least 250 hours; then you have to pass a written test. To get your certificate and look for a job as a pilot, you also have to pass a check-ride. This is like a driving test to get a license, only for a plane. An examiner asks questions, and the pilot-to-be has to plan a flight and fly with the examiner.
> (From http://kids.discovery.com/tell-me/curiosity-corner/
> transportation/how-do-you-become-a-pilot)

Remind students that it is important not to change the meaning or change just one word; they need to rework the sentence to communicate information in a different way.

3. **Full-Class Activity**: Choose a grade-level appropriate short paragraph to read aloud to your students. Tell students they should listen to what you read, try to reword it in their heads to show understanding, and then be ready to share their paraphrasing, getting the main points across. Read the paragraph one time through; have students listen to the big idea first. Then, read the paragraph a second time, moving through one sentence at a time. Have students share ideas for ways to paraphrase each individual sentence. Write down these new paraphrased sentences for the class to see. Continue for each sentence or couple of sentences of the paragraph. Have students then help you reread your paraphrased paragraph. Does it make as much sense? Did you get the main points across? Are there parts of the paraphrased paragraph that can be left out to still give a complete picture of the original paragraph?

4. **Wrap-Up**: Tell students that paraphrasing takes a couple of steps. Students must hear or read the information, comprehend it, and then put that same information

into their own words. Paraphrasing is something they can do when they are reading a text as well as when someone is presenting information to them orally.

Extend the Lesson

The CCSS require that students learn to paraphrase information presented orally, visually, and quantitatively. This lesson focuses on having students paraphrase information presented orally. Once students have a strong grasp of that skill, you can add more lessons on paraphrasing, but next time have students practice paraphrasing information presented in other ways (visually and quantitatively), not just orally.

Differentiation

For students who need extra support
- Give students who need extra support a copy of the paragraph used in the full-class activity. Allow students to work in pairs as they paraphrase each sentence.

For advanced students
- Have advanced students paraphrase paragraphs from their current science textbook in ways that may make the information easier for some students to remember.

Assessment

Check that students understand how to paraphrase a sentence or paragraph. Give students a sample short paragraph about another animal—such information can be found on zoo websites such as that of the San Diego Zoo. Have students write paraphrases of the short paragraph. Do students reword the information? Is pertinent information missing from the paraphrased paragraph? Do the new paragraphs show understanding of the paragraphs students just read? To score students, use the following rubric.

Paraphrase Rubric
Accuracy
3—All information is correct and represents what the original paragraph said.
2—Almost all the key pieces of information are correct.
1—Some information was correct. In some places, the student did not fully understand what was read.
Clarity
3—The paraphrase is easy to understand. All ideas presented in the original paragraph are connected.
2—The information is clearly written, but the thoughts between sentences do not flow.
1—It is difficult to understand the meaning of what is written.
Thoroughness
3—All the sentences are written in the student's words.
2—Most of the sentences are written in the student's words.
1—Some of the sentences are in the student's words. Some are the same as the original paragraph.

Additional Resources

- *Summarizing, Paraphrasing, and Retelling: Skills for Better Reading, Writing, and Test Taking*, by Emily Kissner

- Discovery Kids has a lot of information on different topics and provides some great sample nonfiction text to practice paraphrasing. http://kids.discovery.com/tell-me

Notes

After implementing the lesson, make notes on what worked and what you would change next time.

_____

_____

_____

_____

Hooking 'Em In

Prepare an Oral Report

Grade Levels: 4–5

Time Frame: Approximately one to two class periods

Overview: Students in grades 4–5 are asked to plan and prepare oral presentations that include audio and/or visual components. Teaching students to plan and prepare presentations gives students a skill they will use throughout school and in the real world.

Common Core State Standards

- 4: Speaking and Listening, Standard 4: Report on a topic or text, tell a story, or recount an experience in an organized manner, using appropriate facts and relevant, descriptive details to support main ideas or themes.

- 5: Speaking and Listening, Standard 4: Report on a topic or text or present an opinion, sequencing ideas logically and using appropriate facts and relevant, descriptive details to support main ideas or themes.

- 4: Speaking and Listening, Standard 5: Add audio recordings and visual displays to presentations when appropriate to enhance the development of main ideas or themes.

- 5: Speaking and Listening, Standard 5: Include multimedia components (e.g., graphics, sound) and visual displays in presentations when appropriate to enhance the development of main ideas or themes.

Objectives

- Students will prepare reports on a given topic.

- Students will add appropriate multimedia elements to their presentations, such as audio recordings and visual displays, to enhance the development of the main ideas and themes of the presentations.

Background Knowledge Required

Use of the preferred multimedia equipment (software programs, recording devices, etc.)

Materials Needed

- Copies of the handout: Prepare an Oral Report, p. 148

- A book for each student to use for the report. (Students can report on the same book or use different books.)

- Preferred multimedia equipment (software programs, recording devices, drawing tools, etc.)

Agenda

1. **Introduction**: Tell students that giving an oral report requires preparation. They need to think about the opening of the presentation, the information they want to share, and how they will sum up the presentation. After all, they don't want their listeners to be bored! Students must think about how to make their presentations interesting and clear so people in the audience learn from them.

   Explain to students that they will plan oral presentations on a book they are reading. Planning a report is just as important as giving the report. Point out to students that the more time they spend planning, the fewer errors their presentations will have.

2. **Modeling Activity**: Model for students the planning process. The first step is to brainstorm the important points from the book. On the board, make a list of a few main points from the sample book. Remind students that this is one way of getting ideas down on paper and there is no right or wrong way to brainstorm.

   Next, tell students it is time to pull their brainstorming ideas together and start planning their presentations. They will begin by planning an introduction to the topic geared toward the appropriate audience. This introduction will set the stage so the audience knows what is being presented. Remind students that they wouldn't want to listen to someone talk about something and have to wait until the end of the presentation to figure out what he or she was talking about! The introduction should not be just informative; it should also be interesting. It acts as a hook—something to catch the audience's attention.

   You may want to give an example of a great hook, such as this: "If I were giving a report on *Sarah, Plain and Tall*, I might say something such as 'Have you ever wondered what it would be like to live on a farm? Have you ever wondered what life was like back in the 19th century?' Or 'Have you ever wondered how different life would be if you lost a parent at a young age?' These beginning questions are hooks that get an audience interested. They set the stage and engage the audience in your presentation."

   Explain that the next step after engaging the audience is giving them more information about the book without giving away too much. Remind students not to give away or tell the ending of the book; that would spoil the excitement for readers. Choosing two to four main events that move the story along could help fill in the details for audience members and engage them further.

   Tell students that at the end of the presentation, a good presenter sums up what he or she said. The good presenter does not just repeat but creates a simple summary that highlights his or her opinion and gives the audience a reason to look into the topic further. Explain why a strong finish is important.

   Note: You can break the lesson here, continuing on another day.

3. **Independent Activity**: Pass out the handouts, and tell students to use information about their books to complete the handout. Remind students to brainstorm ideas about what is important from their books. When students are done brainstorming,

they should begin writing their presentations. First, students should write hooks to open their presentations. Then they should choose a few key points to share and write those down. Finally, students should write summary statements that include their opinion of their books and give the audience a reason to check out the books in the future. Allow students time to complete their brainstorming and writing.

4. **Add Multimedia Elements**: After students complete the independent activity, bring them back together as a group. Tell students to think about what else may make their presentations more exciting. Could a visual display, such as a poster of the book that highlights parts of the presentation, excite the audience? Would a PowerPoint presentation be a good support for the oral report? What types of audio recordings might enhance the information in their presentations? Tell students that the next step is to brainstorm a type of multimedia element that could enhance their presentations. As a class, brainstorm ideas of elements students are familiar with, such as any of the following (depending on students' age and experience):

   - Poster
   - Collage
   - Music that matches the theme of the book
   - Drawing or painting of the plot
   - Cartoon drawing of the story
   - Venn diagram comparing and contrasting the characters of the story or of two stories familiar to the audience
   - PowerPoint presentation
   - Kidspiration diagram

   Tell students they will choose ways to visually present their books to the audience that might help pique interest.

   An example you could share with the students related to *Sarah, Plain and Tall* might be to create a poster showing pictures of the seashores of Maine and the wheat fields of the Midwest. A presentation could tell the story of Sarah's move from Maine to the Midwest and use the pictures as a reference for pointing out the differences between the two areas and the struggles Sarah faced with the move.

   Another example for *Sarah, Plain and Tall* would be to share the musical CD that is available on Amazon. You could choose one song or make a recording of bits from all the songs that might help students relate to the story through music.

   Tell students that adding a visual or an audio piece helps place a story in perspective for the audience, giving them something to actually see instead of having to rely on their imaginations. Students should think about a way to enhance their presentations with visual or audio components. Remind students that just as they brainstormed their presentations, they should brainstorm the visual or audio components. Which tool would hook the audience? Which tool could bring the audience to that time or place in history? Which tool could help the audience understand the book more? Those are a few sample questions students could ask themselves as they brainstorm and then prepare their presentations.

5. **Wrap-Up**: Tell students that planning a presentation is just as important as giving the presentation. When presenters lay the groundwork, their presentations go off

without a hitch. Using a planning page, such as the handout used in class, can help organize students' thoughts and pull together everything needed for their reports.

Differentiation

For students who need extra support

- Have students work in pairs on a report of a text. Students can read the same book and then work in pairs to write the report, create the visuals, and eventually give the oral reports. (See Lesson Plan 24, p. 140.)

For advanced students

- Advanced students can mentor or help students who may be struggling to pull together all the pieces for their reports.

- Vary the text difficulty for students based on their reading abilities.

Assessment

Check that students included the three parts in their presentations—a hook or an introduction, information about the text, and a summary statement.

Notes

After implementing the lesson, make notes on what worked and what you would change next time.

_____

_____

_____

_____

Prepare an Oral Report

Plan your oral report! Answer the questions below.

1. What is the name of your book? _____

2. Why should others read this book? _____

   _____

3. Choose three parts of the book you could share to interest the readers without giving away too much of the plot.

   _____

   _____

4. Write one to two sentences that sum up your feelings and opinions about this book. _____

   _____

   _____

   _____

5. Brainstorm ideas for a visual support piece for your presentation. _____

   _____

   _____

Now you're ready to start writing! On separate paper, write out the three parts of your report—a hook, details, and a conclusion.

Putting it All Together

Deliver an Oral Report on a Topic or Text

Grade Levels: 4–5

Time Frame: Approximately one to two class periods

Overview: Students in grades 4–5 are asked to give oral presentations that include audio and/or visual components. This lesson was designed to be used right after Lesson Plan 25, in which students prepared their presentations. In this lesson, students will deliver their presentations.

Common Core State Standards

- 4: Speaking and Listening, Standard 4: Report on a topic or text, tell a story, or recount an experience in an organized manner, using appropriate facts and relevant, descriptive details to support main ideas or themes; speak clearly at an understandable pace.

- 5: Speaking and Listening, Standard 4: Report on a topic or text or present an opinion, sequencing ideas logically and using appropriate facts and relevant, descriptive details to support main ideas or themes; speak clearly at an understandable pace.

- 4: Speaking and Listening, Standard 5: Add audio recordings and visual displays to presentations when appropriate to enhance the development of main ideas or themes.

- 5: Speaking and Listening, Standard 5: Include multimedia components (e.g., graphics, sound) and visual displays in presentations when appropriate to enhance the development of main ideas or themes.

Objectives

- Students will present oral reports on a given topic, speaking clearly and at an understandable pace. They will also make eye contact with the audience and stand with a confident posture.

- Students will use multimedia elements appropriately during their presentations.

Background Knowledge Required

Students should have completed Lesson 25.

Materials Needed

- Completed handout (planning page) and writing from Lesson 25

- Copies of the handout: Rubric for Presenting an Oral Report

Agenda

1. **Introduction**: Tell students that they've done a great job putting together information they would want to share about a book they have just read. The goal today will be to practice giving their oral reports. Remind students that when presenting to an audience, they need to use clear, articulate voices so that the audience can hear and understand the information. Second, presenters need to know what they are going to say so that the information makes sense to the audience. Third, presenters should have practiced so their presentations go smoothly. Fourth, presenters should make eye contact with the audience and show confidence in their ability to share information with others.

2. **Modeling Activity**: As a class, practice these key points for delivering a presentation:

   - Using clear, articulate voices
   - Making eye contact
   - Standing with a confident posture
   - Using multimedia appropriately

   To practice using a clear, articulate voice, start by sharing the following sentence with students in a meek, mumbling voice.

   "Today I will share my presentation on the book *Sarah, Plain and Tall*. This book is a good book that you will like because the author brings you in as if you were in the story with the characters."

   Ask students if they felt you used a clear, articulate voice. Was there any meaning behind the words you shared? Could they understand you? Did what you said interest them? Chances are, if you were meek and mumbling, students will be able to identify that you were not clear and articulate.

   Now say the same sentence again, this time in a clear, articulate voice. Ask students if this changed the meaning of the sentences? Did this excite them about the book? Could they understand you?

   Have students practice saying their introduction sentence(s) to partners in clear, articulate voices. Once students have shown understanding of the type of voice expected in their presentations, move on to modeling the next requirements for the presentation—making eye contact and standing with correct presentation posture. Stand in a slumped position with your head down. Tell students you will share another part of your presentation, and they should be ready to give feedback.

   "*Sarah, Plain and Tall* is set in the 19th century in the midwestern United States. Sarah moves from Maine to the Midwest to become Jacob's wife."

   Ask students what they thought. Could they understand you even though you were using a clear, articulate voice? Did your posture affect their ability to follow along with the presentation? Discuss the importance of standing tall and making eye contact with the audience. Tell students that if they do that, their voices will be clearer and they will sound more articulate.

   Say the statement again, this time focusing on using a clear, articulate voice while making eye contact and standing tall. Discuss with students the difference making eye contact and having correct posture made when sharing the second part of your presentation.

Give students the opportunity to practice another part of their presentation with their partners, this time practicing standing tall, making eye contact, and speaking in a clear, articulate voice.

Note: You can break the lesson here, continuing on another day.

The final skill to model is the ability to use multimedia effectively. Students want technology to enhance their presentations and not distract people from their key points.

The types of multimedia students created will determine how much practice they will need with it. If students are using PowerPoint presentations, they will need time to practice talking and moving through slides. If students created posters, they need to decide whether to share the posters at the beginning of the presentation or at the end. If students plan to use music, they need to figure out whether to use it to introduce the book and set the stage or to use it at the end of the presentation. Have a short discussion about where it might be appropriate for you to share your poster for *Sarah, Plain and Tall,* which shows pictures of Maine and the Midwest. Might you use it at the beginning as you describe the trek Sarah takes? Would it be effective to stop in the middle of the presentation to explain the poster? Should it be explained at the end of the presentation? Help students think through when they will share their multimedia elements.

3. **Small-Group Activity**: Pass out the handout. Walk students through each piece of the rubric, answering any questions they have about the differences between scores. Then allow students time to practice giving their presentations to their partners. Students should focus not only on using clear, articulate voices but also on making eye contact, standing tall, and working out the kinks to make their presentations flow smoothly. Tell students to use the rubric to make sure they are meeting the expectations. Remind students you will use the rubric to evaluate their presentations. During the small group practice, help students troubleshoot any multimedia problems.

Note: You can break the lesson here, continuing on another day.

4. **Full-Class Activity**: Have students share their presentations one at a time in front of the class. Before students begin, remind them of the rubric, the elements you are looking for in their presentations, and the expectations of the rest of the class. The audience should listen attentively, ask questions if appropriate, and be supportive of the presenters. You can even use a separate rubric to assess the audience's attentiveness and support.

5. **Wrap-Up**: Remind students that standing up in front of peers and presenting on a topic is not always the easiest thing to do. Tell them that some adults fear it just as much as some kids do! However, with preparation and planning, it does not have to be so overwhelming. Congratulate students on giving reports on a topic they knew something about and were able to tell others. Remind students that they may have taught someone something new, may have inspired another student, or may have excited someone else to read the book they shared!

Extend the Lesson

Students can plan and present on a topic they know something about or have researched, such as a sport, historical event, or career. The presentations and supporting visual displays can be as simple or elaborate as you want them to be as long as students know the steps of setting up the stage (creating a hook), sharing key information, and summarizing their thoughts and information for the audience.

You may wish/need to spend time on vocabulary, such as *articulate, posture, intonation, enhance, effective, deliver,* etc.

Differentiation

For students who need extra support
- Allow students to create visual support pieces and use them as crutches for the presentation, reading from the slides of a PowerPoint (for example) or explaining the book jacket a student created and using that as the presentation instead of a more formal presentation.

For advanced students
- Allow these students to create more elaborate visual presentation support pieces to accompany their presentations.

Assessment

Use the rubric handout that students practiced from to evaluate each student's presentation.

Additional Resources

- Education World has a great tutorial on introducing PowerPoint to students: www.educationworld.com/a_tech/tech/tech013.shtml.

Notes

After implementing the lesson, make notes on what worked and what you would change next time.

_____

_____

_____

_____

Name: _____   Date: _____

Rubric for Presenting an Oral Report

Use the following rubric to practice your presentation. Circle your answers. Your teacher will use this rubric to evaluate your oral report.

Content

Did the presenter use an effective opening hook for the report?

4—The presenter used an effective hook that made me want to hear more.

3—The presenter included a hook, but it was off topic or unclear.

2—The presenter included an introduction, but it was not exciting.

1—The presenter did not have a hook or introduction.

Did the presenter include enough information about the text and a summarizing statement at the end?

4—The presenter had useful information about the text and a summarizing statement.

3—The presenter had some information about the text and a weak summarizing statement.

2—The presenter had too little information about the text and a weak summarizing statement.

1—The presenter included hardly any information about the text, and the summarizing statement was missing or weak.

Delivery

Was the presenter's voice clear? Were the presenter's volume and pace when speaking appropriate?

4—The presenter used a clear, coherent speaking voice. The volume and pace were appropriate and held the audience's attention.

3—The presenter used a clear speaking voice for most of the presentation. The volume was a little too loud or quiet at times. The speed was a little too slow or fast at times.

2—The presenter was hard to understand for most of the presentation. He (she) spoke too slowly or quickly or was too loud or too quiet.

1—The presenter was not understandable during the presentation.

Did the presenter use a multimedia component effectively?

4—The presenter used an audio (visual) piece well to bring out her (his) important ideas.

3—The presenter used an audio (visual) piece to bring out his (her) important ideas; sometimes the media piece was distracting or unclearly linked to the content.

2—The presenter's use of the media element was distracting or confusing.

1—The presenter barely used or did not use a media component.

Finding Support

Respond to a Speaker's Information

Grade Levels: 4–5

Time Frame: Approximately one class period

Overview: Fourth-grade students are asked to identify information a speaker provides to support particular points he or she makes. Students must pay attention to the speaker and then be able to recall details that were provided and explain how each claim is supported. Fifth-grade students are also asked to identify this information; in addition; fifth graders must summarize the main points. To do this lesson in fourth grade, skip the part about summarizing.

Common Core State Standards

- 4: Speaking and Listening, Standard 3: Identify the reasons and evidence a speaker provides to support particular points.

- 5: Speaking and Listening, Standard 3: Summarize the points a speaker makes and explain how each claim is supported by reasons and evidence.

Objectives

- Students will pay close attention to a speaker and identify his or her reasons and evidence.

- Students will summarize a speaker's main points.

Background Knowledge Required

Fifth graders should be familiar with summary writing. You may wish to refer to the summary-writing lesson on page 117 of this book.

Materials Needed

- Copy of a current events article from a student publication, such as one of Scholastic's classroom magazines, *Time for Kids,* or *National Geographic for Kids,* for each student or on an overhead

- Whiteboard or overhead projector

Agenda

1. **Introduction**: Tell students that when a writer works on an article or a speech, he or she focuses on getting the main points across to the audience. Audience members

must listen to the author or speaker and concentrate on understanding the message being shared. Audience members must be able to recall details presented and the support elements that are given.

Explain that today, students will listen to a current events article read aloud. They should concentrate on the main idea of the article and then listen for a few supporting details the author gives. Tell students you will model what this may look like.

2. **Modeling Activity**: To model this activity, read the following paragraph aloud. You could transfer this paragraph to an overhead or write it on the board for students to refer to as you read. If you wish, substitute a paragraph from another current events article you have access to.

> Most people associate twisters with tornadoes, but in fact tropical twisters come from hurricanes. Hurricanes are what scientists call "strong Tropical Cyclones." They are formed when large areas of the ocean become heated, and the air pressure over that area drops. This causes thunderstorms and strong surface winds. Cyclones develop over tropical or sub-tropical waters (for example, in the Atlantic off the coast of Africa, or in the Pacific). As they travel long distances gathering energy from the ocean, they are likely to be classified as strong Tropical Cyclones. When the winds of a tropical storm reach 74 mph, then the storm is classified as a hurricane. (kids.earth.nasa.gov/archive/hurricane)

Ask students what point the author is trying to make in this paragraph. What message is the author trying to get across? (an explanation of a hurricane)

If students struggle to determine the main idea, reread the passage for students and ask them to concentrate on the big picture.

Once students identify the main idea, ask them for some reasons or evidence the author gives to support that main idea. For example: Warm ocean water and dropping air pressure cause storms. As these storms travel, they become stronger. Hurricanes happen when winds reach 74 mph.

3. **Independent Activity**: Tell students it is now their turn to identify the main point and the reasons and evidence provided. Pass out a copy of a current events article to students, or place an article on an overhead or whiteboard for students to read. Have students take turns reading aloud. Ask students to listen for the reasons and the evidence that support the main idea.

(For fifth graders): Tell students that when they finish reading, they will summarize the point and the supporting reasons and evidence provided. Allow students to use the written article to refer to as they practice this new skill. If necessary, remind students what a summary is.

4. **Wrap-Up**: When students finish their summaries, call on a few students to share with the class. See whether students have differing opinions about the main idea or whether everyone agrees. Tell students that learning to listen to a speaker (or author) and identifying what he or she is saying is a skill they will need in life, such as when working with colleagues on a project. Collect the written summaries for review.

Extend the Lesson

Students could find different articles to share with the class. Have those students read the articles aloud while the rest of the class identifies the main point and the supporting evidence provided. This would require that the students concentrate on listening.

This lesson focuses on listening to the teacher or a student as the speaker, reading something aloud. You could also have students listen to a speech found online as a video or an audio recording and focus on that speaker.

Differentiation

For students who need extra support

- Pull students who are struggling into a small group. Give these students paper copies of the article along with a highlighter and pen to underline. Have students read the article together with you. Then look back through the text, and teach students to find the author's main point. Point out that it is usually at the beginning of a piece, although sometimes it is at the end. Have students highlight the main point. Then ask students to find supporting reasons or evidence. Have the students underline each supporting detail. Then have students work on a second paragraph, highlighting the main point and underlining the details. Once students have shown the ability to identify the key pieces, have them write simple summaries.

For advanced students

- Have students write their own paragraphs about topics that interest them. Have the students write their main points and provide evidence to support their main points. Ask these students to share their writing with the class while the class listens, identifies the main point and evidence, and then summarizes what they heard.

Assessment

Review the written summaries. Have students who did not identify the main point and some evidence to support that point redo the activity with you in a small group setting.

Additional Resources

- Eduplace has a link to current events articles online: www.eduplace.com/ss/current/.

- DOGO News also has a link to current events articles online: www.dogonews.com/.

Notes

After implementing the lesson, make notes on what worked and what you would change next time.

_____

_____

_____

_____

Yo or Hello?

Adapt Speech to a Variety of Contexts and Tasks

Grade Levels: 4–5

Time Frame: Approximately one class period

Overview: The standards require students in grades 4–5 to consider when using formal English is appropriate. Teaching students appropriate ways to adapt their speech to match a variety of contexts and tasks will help students participate in society in a more productive manner.

Common Core State Standards

- 4: Speaking and Listening, Standard 6: Differentiate between contexts that call for formal English (e.g., presenting ideas) and situations where informal discourse is appropriate (e.g., small-group discussion); use formal English when appropriate to task and situation.

- 5: Speaking and Listening, Standard 6: Adapt speech to a variety of contexts and tasks, using formal English when appropriate to task and situation.

- 4: Language, Standard 3c: Differentiate between contexts that call for formal English (e.g., presenting ideas) and situations where informal discourse is appropriate (e.g., small-group discussion).

Objectives

- Students will adapt their speech for a variety of contexts and tasks, such as using formal English when presenting ideas to the class.

Background Knowledge Required

No particular background knowledge is required for this lesson.

Materials Needed

- Copies of the handout, Adapt Speech to a Variety of Contexts and Tasks, p. 161

Agenda

1. **Introduction**: Tell students that today they will talk about the types of language, formal and informal, that are used for different situations. Explain that when talking to a friend, one might use more informal words because that is an accepted practice. However, when giving a presentation to an audience, using formal English is

appropriate. Tell students that knowing when it is appropriate to use formal English vs. informal English is important to learn.

2. **Modeling Activity**: Model for students the differences between formal and informal English. For example, "If I wanted to invite a friend to go to the park after school, what might I say?" Solicit examples from students and write them on the board. Examples may include, "Yo, I'm gonna go to the park after school. Come with."

    Explain that the informal words would never be used in a formal-English setting. Using the above example, you might say, "We'd never use the words *yo* or *gonna* in formal English, but with friends, they are acceptable. If I was going to invite an adult to come to the park after school, what might I say?" Examples may include, "Ma'am, would you like to join me at the park after school today?" Say, "Using a polite expression such as *ma'am* or *sir* is a formal way to address someone." Ask students why formal language is more polite with strangers and other types of people such as a boss at your job or a principal of your school.

    Tell students that adjectives and verbs can be in informal or formal English. An example would be "This homework stinks." vs. "The assigned homework is frustrating."

    Guide students to brainstorm a list of words that may be considered informal English; then brainstorm words that are considered formal English. Write the examples on the board as a reference for the small-group activity. When students show an understanding of formal English examples versus informal English, move on to the small-group activity.

3. **Small-Group Activity**: Organize students into small groups, and pass out the handout to each student. Tell students that they will come up with a formal way of saying something and then an informal way of saying the same thing. Remind students to avoid slang when speaking in formal English, and monitor groups as they work through the different scenarios.

4. **Wrap-Up**: Gather students together, and have each group share a couple of formal and informal ways of saying the same thing (as completed on their handouts). Remind students that knowing what is appropriate in different situations not only makes students sound more intelligent but also helps them be taken more seriously as they learn to navigate different situations.

Extend the Lesson

Have students create scenarios for writing formal and informal statements that say the same thing but use language appropriate to the scenarios.

Differentiation

For students who need extra support

- First, brainstorm words that may be considered informal English, and then brainstorm words that are considered formal English. Monitor the small-group activity, and guide students through the process.

For advanced students

- Give students a passage from a social studies book, and ask them to rewrite the text into informal English, as if they were explaining the information to a friend.

Assessment

Check that students know the difference between formal English and informal English by reviewing their handouts.

Additional Resources

- Many lesson plans are available on how to write a friendly letter. For example, some can be found at EducationWorld (www.educationworld.com/a_lesson/lesson281 .shtml). You can use one of the lessons and adapt it to show students how to go from a more formal letter to a casual e-mail or text message.

Notes

After implementing the lesson, make notes on what worked and what you would change next time.

_____

_____

_____

_____

Adapt Speech to a Variety of Contexts and Tasks

1. When giving an oral report about a book you just read, would you use formal English or informal English during your presentation to your peers? Give an example of how you would write a formal statement about your opinion of this book versus how you would describe it to a friend after school.

   Formal _____

   _____

   Informal _____

   _____

2. Write a formal statement to the cafeteria staff requesting different types of food. Then write an informal statement to your mom about the lunches she packs for you.

   Formal _____

   _____

   Informal _____

   _____

Language

Overview

The Common Core State Standards for Language might seem intimidating for teachers because they require a heavy focus on grammar, which often is not taught explicitly or regularly in schools. The standards lay out which grammar conventions should be taught in each grade level; each year builds on the previous ones. To meet these new grammar requirements, remember that you should not teach grammar in isolation. You do not need to create long, formal units for part of the year. Instead, think of ways you can incorporate grammar mini-lessons into your reading and writing units. Look at your texts and your writing assignments, and see which rules would be a good fit. When you teach a certain convention, you can require students to use it in their own writing, and you can have students look for examples of it in whatever they're reading. Also teach students the "why" behind grammar rules so they see the relevance of clear communication to their own lives.

Along with grammar, vocabulary has a big role in the language standards. Giving students lists of words to memorize does not promote long-term retention. Students will memorize the words for a quiz and forget them days later. Rather, have students spend time uncovering word meanings on their own, relating the word to other words they know, drawing pictures of the word, and so on. Such activities will help students truly learn a word and how to use it accurately. For more tips on revising lessons or creating new lessons, see the checklist below.

Planning Checklist

When planning a CCSS-based language lesson, keep the following tips in mind.

☐ Help students get to know a word rather than simply memorize its definition. For example, you can use graphic organizers to help students come up with examples and non-examples of the word, draw a picture of the word, see how it is similar to and different from a word they already know, etc. Show students how the words are relevant to their lives. As Nancy Sulla (2012) says, information has to have sense and meaning to settle into one's long-term memory. Presenting words in authentic and relevant contexts will ensure that the words make more sense to students (pp. 22–23).

☐ Select words that are widely used and that will help students in school and beyond. Teach content-area words and academic vocabulary rather than the very esoteric words of a story.

☐ Use games and puzzles to build excitement around words.

☐ Teach students how to use context clues and how to understand prefixes and suffixes so they can start to uncover word meanings on their own.

☐ Flood vocabulary instruction throughout the day, rather than saving it for occasional isolated lessons. For example, Debbie Arechiga suggests having a word jar in the classroom. Students can submit new words they find and are curious about. Each day, the teacher chooses one word from the jar to present to students (Arechiga, 2012, p. 170).

☐ Teach students grammar rules, but don't pile on too many at a time. Choose one rule to present during a mini-lesson, and give students ample practice with that rule. The practice should have students apply the rule to their own writing.

☐ Help students learn to think about words and why they are important. How do they help people communicate? How do people select the best words to use? Some words seem similar but have different shades of meaning, some words paint more vivid images than others, some words are more or less formal, etc. Teach students to vary their language depending on the audience and purpose.

☐ Use mentor texts to help students understand different elements of language. In *Awakening Brilliance in the Writer's Workshop,* Lisa Morris offers a list of mentor texts sorted by teaching topics, including adjectives, alliteration, onomatopoeia, beginnings, endings, strong verbs, and sensory details.

Lesson Plans at a Glance

Letters Standing Tall

Use Proper Capitalization

Grade Levels: K–2

Time Frame: Approximately one class period

Overview: Elementary-school students are asked to practice the rules of capitalization in each grade so that by the time they leave fifth grade, they have a strong command of English and the rules of capitalization in writing. This lesson focuses on how to introduce capitalization rules to students in the early elementary grades, K–2.

Common Core State Standards
- K: Language, Standard 2: Demonstrate command of the conventions of standard English capitalization, punctuation, and spelling when writing. a. Capitalize the first word in a sentence and the pronoun *I*.

- 1: Language, Standard 2: Demonstrate command of the conventions of standard English capitalization, punctuation, and spelling when writing. a. Capitalize dates and names of people.

- 2: Language, Standard 2: Demonstrate command of the conventions of standard English capitalization, punctuation, and spelling when writing. a. Capitalize names of holidays, product names, and geographic names.

Objectives
- Students will identify capitalization errors in written sentences.

- Students will write simple sentences using correct capitalization.

Background Knowledge Required
Students need to be able to write a simple, grade-level appropriate sentence.

Materials Needed
- Copies of handout: Use Correct Capitalization, p. 169

Agenda
1. **Introduction**: Tell students that capitalizing letters is an important part of learning to write. Today they will learn about when to use capital letters. All sentences begin with capital letters, and the pronoun *I* is always capitalized. The names of people, days of the week, and months of the year are also capitalized. In addition, the names

of holidays, certain products, and geographic places are capitalized. Learning these simple rules will become lifelong tools. Choose how much to say depending on the requirement of that grade-level standard listed on the previous page.

On the board, list the grade-level appropriate rule for capitalizing that you will work on today. For example, kindergarten teachers would write "first word of a sentence and pronoun *I*."

2. **Modeling Activity**: On the board, write a few sample sentences that are missing the correct punctuation. If you are teaching kindergarten, include sentences with *I* and sentences that do not start with capital letters. Here are a few sample sentences for each grade level:

   Kindergarten:
   the boy ran to the park.
   jump up and down with me.
   he and i went swimming.

   First grade:
   We start school on monday.
   bob and sam swam in the river.
   kim's favorite month is june.

   Second grade:
   I am thankful for thanksgiving.
   What is your favorite crayola crayon color?
   new york city is a busy and beautiful city.

   Tell students that the sentences need some help with capitalization. Call on students to help you find the errors, pointing out and reinforcing the capitalization rule that needs correction. Tell students it is now their turn to write sentences using correct capitalization.

3. **Independent Activity**: Pass out the handout for this lesson. For kindergarten students, encourage inventive spelling using a capital letter at the beginning of a sentence. If kindergarten students are not ready to do their own inventive spellings, do a group write in which everyone writes the same sentence together, focusing on using a capital letter at the beginning of the sentence. For first and second graders, have students write simple sentences using capitals where appropriate for the grade-level standards.

4. **Wrap-Up**: Organize students into pairs, and have students share their sentences with their partners. Does each sentence follow the capitalization rules for that grade level? Have students point to their partners' capital letters. Kindergarten students would point to the beginning word of the sentence. First graders would point to the names of people, days, and months, along with the beginning word in the sentence. In second grade, students would point to holiday names, certain product names, and geographic names used in the sentences, along with any dates and names of people and the first word of a sentence.

Then choose a few students to share their sentences. Write the sentences on the board and point out the correct capitalization rule they followed by circling the correct capital letter(s).

Extend the Lesson

Have students write their own sentences without prompts. Students can write their correct sentences on the board and have other students point out how they used capital letters correctly.

Differentiation

For students who need extra support

- Use the handout in a small group, and have students complete the sentences together.

- Give students sentences to write instead of having them come up with their own sentences.

For advanced students

- Have the advanced students write multiple sentences for each prompt instead of just one.

- Pair a struggling student with an advanced student to write sentences together. Advanced students can mentor students who are struggling to use the capitalization rules.

Assessment

To check students' understanding, collect the handouts and check sentences for correct capitalization. Help students understand their mistakes.

Additional Resources

- A number of daily oral language books are available through a variety of publishers and on www.amazon.com. The basis of daily oral language is to correct and discuss two sentences daily and review and maintain punctuation, capitalization, usage, and writing skills while developing and practicing proofreading skills.

Notes

After implementing the lesson, make notes on what worked and what you would change next time.

_____

_____

_____

_____

Use Correct Capitalization

1. Write a sentence about your favorite day.

_____

_____

_____

2. Write a sentence about your favorite place to visit.

_____

_____

_____

3. Write a sentence about a holiday.

_____

_____

_____

Punctuation Station

How End Punctuation Functions

Grade Level: 1; can be modified to introduce punctuation in kindergarten or review it with students at higher grade levels.

Time Frame: Approximately four class periods

Overview: The standards require elementary school students to learn the basic rules of punctuation. In kindergarten, students should be able to name end punctuation. In first grade, students should use end punctuation correctly. By the end of fifth grade, students should be writing clear, coherent sentences using appropriate end punctuation. This lesson plan focuses on first grade, when students should be getting a handle on how to use end punctuation correctly. The lesson plan is broken into a series of four mini-lessons you can use as students work on a narrative, an opinion-based essay, or other writing assignment for your class.

Common Core State Standards

- 1: Language, Standard 2: Demonstrate command of the conventions of standard English capitalization, punctuation, and spelling when writing. b. Use end punctuation for sentences.

Objectives

- Students will write sentences using correct end punctuation.
- Students will edit their writing for proper use of end punctuation.

Background Knowledge Required

Students need to be able to read and write grade-level appropriate sentences.

Materials Needed

- *Punctuation Takes a Vacation*, by Robin Pulver
- *If You Were an Exclamation Point*, by Shelly Lyons
- Sentence strips and pocket chart (or you can write the sentences on the board)
- Copies of a writing assignment that students are working on in class.

Agenda

Introduction: Introduce students to ending punctuation marks. Read the story *Punctuation Takes a Vacation*, by Robin Pulver. After reading the story, tell students that all sentences end with one of three punctuation marks. The goal for each mini-lesson is to learn about one of the three punctuation marks. Tell students that on the fourth day, they will review each type of punctuation mark.

Day 1: Periods

1. **Instruction:** Explain periods to students. Tell students a period is a small dot used to end a sentence that tells something. Write the following sample sentences on the board without their punctuation:

   - My mom is kind
   - I like the color red
   - Apples grow on trees

   Point out to students that these sentences are all statements, so each needs a period at the end. Write a period at the end of each statement.

   Read the sentences aloud and point out how your voice doesn't go up as it does when you ask a question; it stays matter-of-fact. When reading these types of sentences aloud, students should not raise their voices at the end. Read a couple of the sample sentences aloud as a group.

2. **Modeling Activity:** Tell students that today they will add end punctuation to sentences. Remind students to use a period if a sentence tells something.

   Write the following sentences on sentence strips. On separate sentence strips, write periods. Place one sentence in the pocket chart. Have the students read the sentence and determine if it is a telling sentence. If it is, place one of the periods at the end of the sentence. Repeat for each of the sentences. Call on students to add the periods to the sentences to keep this portion more interactive.

   I want that toy
   The mountain has snow on top
   Swimming is fun
   The frog can jump
   John likes running
   My dad says the sky is always blue

3. **Writing Application:** Have students take out an essay they are writing for class and see where they put the periods. Have students check if they left out any or made any mistakes with periods. Have students read some of their telling statements to a partner or to the full class.

Day 2: Question Marks

1. **Instruction:** Tell students that they will learn about a different ending punctuation mark. Take a moment and review that a period is used at the end of a telling sentence. Ask students what might be used at the end of an asking sentence. Introduce students to the question mark. Write one on the board, and ask students if they know what this mark is. Tell students that a question mark is used at the end of a sentence that asks a question. Write the following sentences on the board without question marks.

   - What day is today
   - Where do you live
   - What is your favorite food

Point out to students that these sentences ask questions, so they should end in question marks. Read the sentences, modeling the change in vocal intonation to indicate the question, and then write a question mark at the end of each statement.

Now have students read aloud the sentences along with you. Show students how their inflection changes to ask a question.

2. **Modeling Activity**: Tell students that they are going to add end punctuation to sentences. Remind students to use question marks with asking sentences.

Write the following sentences on sentence strips. On separate sentence strips, write periods and question marks. Place one sentence in the pocket chart. Have the students read the sentence and determine whether it is an asking sentence. If it is, place one of the question marks at the end of the sentence. Repeat for each sentence. Call on students to add the question marks to the sentences to keep this portion more interactive. Keep the periods available to see whether students can tell the difference between the two types of sentences they have learned about so far: telling and asking.

- Can we go to the park
- Let's eat lunch at Joe's Pizza
- What time is bedtime
- How do you jump like that
- Sarah is coming to the party
- Why is the elephant so big
- The field trip is on Friday

Have the students read each sentence aloud with the punctuation mark. When a sentence is asking something, ask students to change their voice (intonation) to show that.

3. **Writing Application**: Have students take out an essay they are writing for class and see where they put the question marks. If they don't have any questions in their writing, have them add one or two. Have students check if they left out any or made any mistakes with question marks. Have students read some of their questions to a partner or to the full class.

Day 3: Exclamation Points
1. **Instruction:** Read the book *If You Were an Exclamation Point,* by Shelly Lyons. Then explain to students that an exclamation point is used at the end of a sentence that expresses a strong emotion. An exclamation point is a straight line with a small period underneath it. Write the following sentences on the board without the exclamation points.

- I am mad at you
- Get up
- Fire
- You're wonderful

Point out to students that all of these sentences are telling something and that adding an exclamation point shows a strong emotion about the message. Read the sentences again, and add exclamation points on the board. Model for students how to read these sentences with passion and emotion. If students are ready, erase the exclamation points and put periods. Read the sentences again, this time without strong emotion. Tell students that an exclamation point tells readers how to read a sentence and changes the meaning because there is more emotion behind the sentence.

2. **Modeling Activity**: Tell students that they will add end punctuation to sentences. Remind students to use an exclamation point if a sentence shows strong emotion.

   Write the following sentences on sentence strips. On separate sentence strips, write periods, question marks, and exclamation points. Place one sentence in the pocket chart. Have the students read the sentence and determine whether it shows strong emotion. If it does, place an exclamation point at the end of the sentence. Repeat for each sentence. Call on students to add exclamation points to sentences to keep this portion more interactive. Keep the periods and question marks available to see if students can tell the difference between the different types of sentences they have learned about so far: telling, asking, and showing strong emotion.

   Why is your brother laughing
   I want that toy now
   My sister's name is Sophia
   May I have a piece of cake
   Leave me alone
   My favorite hobby is making jewelry

   Have the students read each sentence aloud with the punctuation mark. Ask students to change their voices when a sentence shows strong emotion.

   Tell students that sentences 2, 3, and 6 (above) are telling sentences and could have periods at the end. Place a period at the end of each of those sentences instead of the exclamation point. Read each sentence without the strong emotion. Does the sentence mean the same thing? Have students determine which way is more powerful and makes the most sense for each sentence—the period or the exclamation point?

3. **Writing Application**: Have students take out an essay they are writing for class and see where they put any exclamation marks. If they don't have any exclamation marks in their writing, have them add one or two. Have students check if they left out any or made any mistakes with exclamation marks. Have students read some of their exclamatory statements to a partner or to the full class.

Day 4: Punctuation Review
1. **Instruction:** Remind students that they have now learned about all the different types of ending punctuation marks. If time allows, reread *Punctuation Takes a Vacation*. Stop as necessary to point out the different types of end punctuation to students. This will be a great reminder of the importance of each type of end punctuation mark.

   Tell students that today they will review all three types of ending punctuation: period, question mark, and exclamation point. Review each type of punctuation and the type of sentence it matches: periods are for telling sentences, question marks are for questions, and exclamation points are for sentences that show strong emotion.

Write on the board or place in the pocket chart each type of ending punctuation for students to reference throughout the lesson.

2. **Modeling Activity**: Tell students that they will add end punctuation to different kinds of sentences. Write the following sentences on sentence strips. On separate sentence strips, write periods, question marks, and exclamation points. Place one sentence in the pocket chart. Have the students read the sentence and determine what type of sentence it is and what the appropriate ending punctuation mark is. If students are unsure, try out multiple ending punctuation marks, reading the sentence aloud and determining from there which punctuation mark is most effective.

Can I call my friend
This water is freezing cold
I like sitting under the shady tree
Look out for that hole
When will we be done
I want to go to the beach

Have the students read each sentence aloud with the punctuation mark. Ask students to change their voice to show that the sentence is a telling something, asking a question, or showing strong emotion. If students appear to be struggling with one particular type of end punctuation, add more sentences of that type. Have students go back to their writing and reread it one last time to make sure that all of their sentences end with the proper end punctuation. If time allows, students can swap essays with a peer and check one another's work.

3. **Wrap-Up**: Remind students that from now on they should end every sentence with the appropriate ending punctuation mark.

Differentiation

For students who need extra support
- Use the handout in a small group, and have students complete the sentences together.

For advanced students
- Pair a struggling student with an advanced student. They can write sentences together, and the advanced student can mentor the other student to use the correct end punctuation.

Assessment

When you assess students' essays, evaluate their use of end punctuation.

Additional Resources

- *Punctuation Celebration,* by Elsa Knight Bruno—children's book of punctuation poetry

- *Penny and the Punctuation Bee,* by Moira Rose Donahue—children's book about punctuation

- *Twenty-Odd Ducks,* by Lynda Truss—children's book about punctuation

Notes

After implementing the lesson, make notes on what worked and what you would change next time.

_____

_____

_____

_____

Getting Down
the Bare Bones

Writing Simple Sentences

Grade Levels: K–1; can be easily adapted to grades 2 and 3 (see note in Overview)

Time Frame: Approximately two class periods

Overview: The Common Core Language Standards require students in grades K–5 to write complete sentences. In the early grades, the focus is on writing simple sentences that use correct capitalization and punctuation. By the upper grades, students should be confident writing more advanced sentences. This lesson, designed for grades K–1, teaches how to form simple sentences with nouns and verbs. You can adapt this lesson to higher grades by briefly reviewing nouns and verbs and then teaching students how to form expanded sentences with adjectives and adverbs. (Use the same activities in this lesson but add adjective/adverb cards to the noun and verb cards.)

Common Core State Standards

- K: Language, Standard 1: Demonstrate command of the conventions of standard English grammar and usage when writing or speaking. b. Use frequently occurring nouns and verbs.

- 1: Language, Standard 1: Demonstrate command of the conventions of standard English grammar and usage when writing or speaking. b. Use common, proper, and possessive nouns. c. Use singular and plural nouns with matching verbs in basic sentences (e.g., *He Hops*; *We hop*).

- 1: Speaking and Listening, Standard 6: Produce complete sentences when appropriate to task and situation.

Objectives

- Students will understand how nouns and verbs make sentences.

- Students will write simple sentences using standard English.

Background Knowledge Required

No particular background knowledge is required for this lesson.

Materials Needed

- *If You Were a Noun,* by Dahl, Michael, and Gray or *A Mink, A Fink, A Skating Rink: What Is a Noun?*, by Brian P. Cleary and Jenya Prosmitsky

- *Nouns and Verbs Have a Field Day*, by Robin Pulver

- *To Root, To Toot, To Parachute: What Is a Verb?*, by Brian P. Cleary and Jenya Prosmitsky or *If You Were a Verb*, by Dahl, Michael, and Gray

- Sentence strips or index cards

- Pocket chart

- Copies of the handout: Forming Simple Sentences, p. 180

- Scissors for each student

Agenda

1. **Introduction**: Tell students that writing sentences requires two things: nouns and verbs. Tell students that nouns are the people, places, or things in a sentence. Then tell students that verbs are the actions the people or things do.

2. **Introduce Nouns**: Read either *If You Were a Noun* or *A Mink, A Fink, A Skating Rink: What is a Noun?* to your students. Use one of these books to pique students' interest in nouns.

   As a group, define nouns and create a list of common nouns. You may want to make three columns on the board of people, places, and things and put the sample nouns in the correct columns. If students have difficulty creating a list of words, go column by column. Create a list of people, then a list of places, and then a list of things. Point out items in the classroom that are nouns. Once students show understanding of nouns, introduce them to verbs.

3. **Introduce Verbs**: Read either *To Root, To Toot, To Parachute: What Is a Verb?* or *If You Were a Verb*. Use one of these books to pique students' interest in verbs.

   As a group, define verbs and create a list of common verbs. If students struggle coming up with sample words, ask them about their favorite sports, their favorite outdoor activities, their favorite indoor activities, or their favorite things to do on the playground. This should give them ideas for the list. If students continue to struggle, give them two words, such as *dog* and *jump*. Ask them which word they can do—can they dog or can they jump? This is a good tool to help students understand the difference between nouns and verbs.

4. **Introduce Sentences**: Tell students that all sentences need at least one noun and one verb. For example, the sentence "The dog ran." has both a noun and a verb. *Dog* is a noun and *ran* is the verb—what the dog did. Tell students that words such as *he, she, I, they,* and *them* or people's names can be used in place of nouns. Give the example that a sentence can be as simple as two words:

   - Dogs run.
   - Girls swim.
   - He laughs.
   - I dream.

   Point out that all of these are very simple sentences but are considered true sentences because each has a noun and a verb. You can also give examples of what doesn't make a sentence and ask students what they could add to make it a sentence.

5. **Full-Class Activity**: Write six nouns on individual sentence strips or index cards, for example, *Max, Sarah, Mom, Dad, Bunny, Dogs*. Capitalize the first letter of each word. Now write six verbs on individual sentence strips or index cards, for example, *giggles, swims, relaxes, sleeps, reads, sits*. Use only lowercase letters.

   Write six periods on separate index cards or sentence strips. You now have the elements for creating sentences in the pocket chart with students.

   Place one of the capitalized nouns in the pocket chart. Show students the verbs, and, as a group, choose one to go with the noun to complete the sentence. Add a period to the end, and read the sentence aloud as a group. Ask students, "In this sentence, is a person doing something? If so, it is a complete sentence."

   Continue creating simple sentences that have one noun and one verb.

   Using the sentence strips or index cards in the pocket chart, work together as a class to create simple sentences that have one noun and one verb.

   Note: You can break the lesson here and continue the next day.

6. **Partner Activity**: Organize students into pairs. Pass out the handout, scissors, pencils, and paper. The handout lists nouns and verbs. Have students cut out their cards and put their nouns in a pile, their verbs in a pile, and their periods in a pile.

   Have students work with their partners to create simple noun-verb sentences with their cards, manipulating their cards the way you demonstrated in the full-class activity. Have students write five bare-bones sentences with their partners.

7. **Writing Application**: Give students an opinion-writing prompt, such as "My favorite book is . . ." Have students write five simple sentences in response to the prompt.

8. **Wrap-Up:** If time allows, you can read *Nouns and Verbs Have a Field Day* to sum up the importance of nouns and verbs in simple sentences.

Extend the Lesson

For second graders (and ready first graders), introduce the concept of adding adjectives and adverbs. You can add a page of adjectives and adverbs to the handout and have students create expanded sentences.

Differentiation

For students who need extra support

▪ Complete the handout in a small group. Guide students to write the same sentence instead of doing the partner activity without adult support.

For advanced students

▪ Have students add places to their sentences or rearrange their sentences so they are not as simple as the examples worked through in the full-class activity.

▪ Advanced students can be given blank cards to fill in their own nouns and verbs to use with the nouns and verbs on the handout.

Assessment

To check students' understanding, have them turn in their sentences from the partner activity. Check the sentences for completeness. Also assess students' writing in response to the prompt.

Additional Resources

- The website havefunteaching.com/songs/grammar-songs/noun-song has a number of songs to teach nouns, verbs, and other language arts topics. For some students, a song is a great hook to learn something new.

- *Many Luscious Lollipops (World of Language),* by Ruth Heller

- *Things That Are Most in the World,* by Judi Barrett

- *The Maestro Plays,* by Bill Martin

- *Suddenly Alligator,* by Rick Walton

- *Up, Up and Away,* by Ruth Heller

Notes

After implementing the lesson, make notes on what worked and what you would change next time.

_____

_____

_____

_____

Forming Simple Sentences

Nouns and Verbs. Cut out these cards, and sort them into three piles—nouns, verbs, and periods. Then form sentences with the words and punctuation.

A boy	A girl	.
runs	skips	.
shops	Tom	.
Jill	.	jumps
writes	.	Ella

Sentence Power

Forming Compound Sentences

Grade Level: 3; can be adapted to other grades (see note in Overview)

Time Frame: Approximately one or two class periods

Overview: This lesson teaches students how to form compound sentences by using simple sentences and conjunctions. You can use this lesson in conjunction with a writing assignment to help students apply what they learn about sentences (e.g., as a revision mini-lesson). This lesson was written for third graders, but you can adapt it to other elementary grades by using simpler or more challenging sentences and by spending more or less time on the proper punctuation of compound sentences.

Common Core State Standards

- 3: Language, Standard 1: Demonstrate command of the conventions of standard English grammar and usage when writing or speaking. h. Use coordinating and subordinating conjunctions. i. Produce simple, compound, and complex sentences.

- 3: Language, Standard 2: Demonstrate command of the conventions of standard English capitalization, punctuation, and spelling when writing.

- 3: Language, Standard 6: Acquire and accurately use grade-appropriate conversational, general academic, and domain-specific words and phrases.

- 3: Writing, Standard 5: With guidance and support from peers and adults, develop and strengthen writing as needed by planning, revising, and editing.

Objectives

- Students will learn how to produce compound sentences by using simple sentences and coordinating conjunctions.

- Students will use their knowledge of compound sentences to revise their writing for sentence variety.

Background Knowledge Required

Students should have a basic understanding of producing sentences, including beginning a sentence with a capital letter and ending it with end punctuation.

Materials Needed

- Handout: Compound Sentences Activity Sheet, p. 184

- Examples of students' writing

Agenda

1. **Introduction and Modeling**: Write this paragraph on the board:

    > I will never forget Kyra's birthday. I arrived at her house early. Her mom let me in. I looked around. I didn't see Kyra. Where was everybody? I was early. They were late. With a sigh, I sat on a chair near the party table. I felt something squishy underneath me. I jumped up. Oh, no! I had sat on the cake!

    Explain that this paragraph is made up of *simple sentences*. This means that each sentence has one independent clause and no dependent clauses. (You can take time to review clauses, subjects, and verbs, but a review is not essential to this lesson.)

    Read the paragraph aloud, drawing attention to the choppy sound of the series of short, simple sentences. Tell students that they can revise the paragraph so that it has some simple sentences and some compound sentences. A *compound sentence* is made up of two simple sentences. The simple sentences are connected with a comma and a conjunction (*and, but, or, nor, for, yet*). List the conjunctions on the board, and have the class read aloud each word with you.

    Note: The Common Core State Standards don't ask students to focus on using commas with coordinating conjunctions until grade 4, but it's worth including in this lesson even if you don't grade students on this comma usage.

2. **Mini-Lesson**: Pass out paper and pencils. Using the sentences on the board, explain and demonstrate how to use a comma and a coordinating conjunction to combine two simple sentences. Ask students to copy each compound sentence that you form. Point out that a writer should combine two sentences only when they are closely related in meaning. Tell students that some of the simple sentences in this paragraph do not need to be combined with another sentence. Give them this example of how they might combine sentences:

    > I will never forget Kyra's birthday. I arrived at her house early, **and** her mom let me in. I looked around, **but** I didn't see Kyra. Where was everybody? I was early, **or** they were late. With a sigh, I sat on a chair near the party table. I felt something squishy underneath me, **and** I jumped up. Oh, no! I had sat on the cake!

    Point out that a writer does three things when using two simple sentences to form a compound sentence: strike out the period and add a comma, add a conjunction, and (usually) change an uppercase letter to lowercase. (That is not necessary when the second simple sentence starts with the pronoun *I* or a proper noun.) Have students check their copies of your work to see if they did these three things.

    Note: You can break the lesson here, continuing on another day.

3. **Independent Work**: Pass out the handout, and go over the instructions. Have students complete the handout.

4. **Wrap-Up**: Have students go back to a piece of their own writing (a report, a blog entry, or just a paragraph) and read it, looking at their sentences. Which simple sentences could they combine? Have them make notes to use when writing their final drafts or revise a shorter piece right away.

Extend the Lesson

- Throughout the year, have students routinely use compound sentences as they complete writing assignments in your class.

- Have students identify compound sentences in a text they are reading. Have them take apart compound sentences to form simple sentences. Compare the two versions. Ask: Which version makes the connections between ideas clearer? Why?

Differentiation

For students who need extra support

- In the wrap-up activity, have students workshop their revisions with partners who can provide extra help.

- Retype the handout so that the sentences are in list form as opposed to paragraph form. Guide students to bracket three pairs of simple sentences that can be combined to form compound sentences. Ask volunteers to suggest which conjunctions might work best. Then have students write the compound sentences independently.

For advanced students

- As part of the mini-lesson, ask volunteers to combine simple sentences that you write on the board. With each example, ask a different volunteer to point out the three things the writer did: strike out the period and add a coma, add a conjunction, and change an uppercase letter to lowercase if needed.

Assessment

- Check students' work on the handout. Possible answers are these:

  1. I set out two pieces of bread, **and** I spread on peanut butter.
  2. I would rather pack a slice of pizza, **but** my mom won't let me.
  3. Then I wash an apple, **or** I grab a banana.

- For the wrap-up activity, evaluate whether students were able to revise their writing based on what they learned during the mini-lesson. You can include the use of compound sentences on the rubric you use to assess their final drafts.

Additional Resources

The following site suggests games that help students practice compound sentences: www.ehow.com/info_8450389_games-compound-sentences.html

Notes

After implementing the lesson, make notes on what worked and what you would change the next time.

_____

_____

_____

_____

Compound Sentence Activity Sheet

This paragraph includes only simple sentences. Some of the ideas in the sentences are closely connected. Combine some of the simple sentences to make compound sentences. You should have **three** compound sentences. Write your three compound sentences on the lines that follow.

When you combine sentences, be sure to do three things:

1. Take away the period, and add a comma.
2. Add a conjunction: *and, but, or, nor, for,* or *yet.*
3. Look at the word after the conjunction. Change the capital letter to a lowercase letter if you need to. You don't need to if the word is *I* or a proper noun, such as someone's name.

Sometimes I make my own lunch for school. I set out two pieces of bread. I spread on peanut butter. I would rather pack a slice of pizza. My mom won't let me. Then I wash an apple. I grab a banana. I pack some string cheese and maybe some crackers. Most important, I choose a dessert.

Compound sentences:

1. _____

   _____

2. _____

   _____

3. _____

   _____

Reuse and Recycle Words!

Multiple-Meaning Words

Grade Level: 3; easily adaptable to other grade levels (see note in Overview)

Time Frame: Approximately one or two class periods

Overview: Students are asked to learn multiple-meaning words from kindergarten onward. With that in mind, you can adapt this lesson to any elementary grade level by choosing a list of multiple-meaning words that your students need to learn or review. For grades K and 1, omit the use of the dictionary and increase the emphasis on drawing pictures to help convey meaning.

Common Core State Standards

- 3: Language, Standard 4: Determine or clarify the meaning of unknown and multiple-meaning words and phrases based on *grade 3 reading and content*, choosing flexibly from a range of strategies. a. Use sentence-level context as a clue to the meaning of a word or phrase. d. Use glossaries or beginning dictionaries, both print and digital, to determine or clarify the precise meaning of key words and phrases.

- 3: Language, Standard 6: Acquire and accurately use grade-appropriate conversational, general academic, and domain-specific words and phrases.

- 3: Writing, Standard 4: With guidance and support from adults, produce writing in which the development and organization are appropriate to task and purpose.

- 3: Writing, Standard 10: Write routinely over extended time frames (time for research, reflection, and revision) and shorter time frames (a single sitting or a day or two) for a range of discipline-specific tasks, purposes, and audiences.

- 3: Speaking and Listening, Standard 4: Report on a topic or text, tell a story, or recount an experience with appropriate facts and relevant, descriptive details, speaking clearly at an understandable pace.

Objectives

- Students will review the concept of multiple-meaning words.

- Students will determine the meanings of multiple-meaning words using dictionaries and prior knowledge.

- Students will write sentences and paragraphs to demonstrate correct use of multiple-meaning words in context.

Background Knowledge Required

From their work in second grade, students should be familiar with the concept of multiple-meaning words.

Materials Needed

- Dictionaries (one per student)

- Copies of handout: Multiple-Meaning Words Activity Sheet, p. 190

Agenda

1. **Introduction**: Pass out the paper and pencils, and write the word *bat* on the board. Ask students to write a sentence that tells something about a bat. Don't answer questions such as "Do you mean a baseball bat?" or "Do you mean a bat that flies?" Just restate your instructions to write a sentence.

   Ask five or six volunteers to read their sentences so that students see that *bat* can mean a piece of sporting equipment or a flying mammal. If someone uses *bat* as a verb, that's okay too. Tell students that words such as *bat* are multiple-meaning words. This means they have more than one meaning. Readers need to see the word in a sentence to know how a writer or speaker is using the word.

2. **Partner Work**: Write a list of multiple-meaning words on the board. Suggestions are *saw, ball, sheet, bank, fall, glass, border,* and *swallow.* Organize students into pairs and assign each pair a word. Pass out copies of the handout and dictionaries. Have each pair of students complete the handout using their assigned word, the dictionary, and their own knowledge.

3. **Full-Class Discussion**: Have pairs share their results with the class. Clarify or correct their findings if necessary.

   Note: You can break the lesson here, continuing on another day.

4. **Wrap-Up**: The Common Core emphasizes the importance of placing skills and knowledge in the larger context of reading and writing. With this in mind, for homework or an in-class assignment, have students write short articles for a class portfolio. The theme of the portfolio is Facts and Fiction. Each student must write a text that uses a multiple-meaning word to show at least two meanings of the word. The purpose of the text is *either* to give information (fact) or to tell a story (fiction). Students should choose the purpose of their writing. If they are learning keyboarding skills, ask them to type their articles. Staple the articles together, and display the portfolio in the classroom so that students can read it during free time.

Extend the Lesson

Give students a week to collect as many multiple-meaning words as they can. Have them keep a log that lists each word, where they read it or heard it, its meaning, and how it could be used to mean something different. To incorporate speaking and listening standards, have each student use his or her notes to teach one multiple-meaning word to the class. You could spread this activity out over days or weeks.

Differentiation

For students who need extra support

- On a poster or chart page, complete a model of the handout using a word that is not part of the assignment. Walk students through an examination of each piece of information in the model. Or create a blank model, and think aloud as you complete it as a demonstration.

For advanced students

- Organize students into pairs, and give them the option of completing a second handout using words they choose from your list or their own knowledge.

Assessment

- Give students a fresh copy of the handout and ask them to complete it independently to show you what they have learned about multiple-meaning words. You can provide a list of word choices or ask advanced students to find words on their own.

- Use this rubric to assess the wrap-up writing activity. A top-score response earns 12 points.

Task	Choose One	Score
The student uses a multiple-meaning word.	novice: (1 point), proficient: (2 points), advanced: (3 points)	
The student writes text that demonstrates a correct meaning of the word.	novice: (1 point), proficient: (2 points), advanced: (3 points)	
The student writes text that demonstrates a second correct meaning of the word.	novice: (1 point), proficient: (2 points), advanced: (3 points)	
The student writes a narrative or informative text, as directed.	novice: (1 point), proficient: (2 points), advanced: (3 points)	
	Total Points:	

Additional Resources

Lists of multiple-meaning words are available online, such as this page from SLP Lesson Plans: http://slplessonplans.com/files/mmwlist.pdf. Look for lists that include words that can function as multiple-meaning nouns or verbs as opposed to lists that simply list words that can be nouns or verbs; though helpful, the latter kind of list limits a full understanding of the concept.

Notes

After implementing the lesson, make notes on what worked and what you would change next time.

_____

_____

_____

_____

Multiple-Meaning Words Activity Sheet

Write a multiple-meaning word on the line at the top. Then fill out the chart to show two different meanings of the word. If the word has more than two meanings, choose the two meanings that you use most often.

word: _____

Meaning 1	**Meaning 2**
Part of speech: _____	Part of speech: _____
Definition: _____ _____ _____	Definition: _____ _____ _____
Used in a sentence: _____ _____ _____ _____	Used in a sentence: _____ _____ _____ _____
Memory clue or picture clue to word's meaning:	Memory clue or picture clue to word's meaning:

Piece by Piece, This Word Makes Sense

Roots, Prefixes, and Suffixes

Lesson Plan 34

Grade Level: 4; easily adaptable to grades 3 and 5 (see note in Overview)

Time Frame: Approximately one or two class periods

Overview: This lesson reviews the terms *prefix, suffix,* and *root* and goes on to teach a select set of words containing a prefix, a suffix, or both types of affixes. Students also learn to use a dictionary to check the meanings of word parts and to link new words to prior knowledge. To adapt the lesson to a different grade level, select your own key words to use in the lesson and activities.

Common Core State Standards

- 4: Language, Standard 4: Determine or clarify the meanings of unknown and multiple-meaning words and phrases based on *grade 4 reading and content*, choosing flexibly from a range of strategies. b. Use common, grade-appropriate Greek and Latin affixes and roots as clues to the meaning of a word (e.g., *telegraph, photograph, autograph*). c. Consult reference materials (e.g., dictionaries, glossaries, thesauruses), both print and digital, to find the pronunciation and determine or clarify the precise meaning of key words and phrases.

Objectives

- Students will determine or clarify the meanings of unfamiliar words by using knowledge of affixes and roots.

- Students will consult print or digital dictionaries to determine or clarify the meaning of an affix, a root, or a word.

Background Knowledge Required

Students should be familiar with the concepts of word roots, prefixes, and suffixes; however, this lesson reviews these terms.

Materials Needed

- Dictionaries (print or digital; one per student)

- Copies of handout: Word Parts Activity Sheet, p. 194

Agenda

1. **Introduction**: To review the concepts prefix, suffix, and word root, write a couple of model words on the board. You might use *microcosm* and *cosmic.* The Greek root

cosm means "universe." The prefix *micro-* means "very small." The suffix *-ic* means "pertaining to." Have students use their knowledge of the root *cosm* to make educated guesses about the meanings of the terms listed below. Have fun with it rather than pushing students for rigid "correct" definitions. Just help them use their knowledge that *cosm* means "universe" to play around with ideas.

- cosmic dust (scientific definition: "fine particles of matter in space"; informal definition: "dust of the universe")
- cosmic time (the time covered by the life of the universe)
- cosmic joke (a trick the universe plays)
- cosmic noise (radio-frequency noise that comes from outside Earth's atmosphere)

As students speculate about the meanings of the above phrases, link their ideas to larger contexts. Ask questions such as, "If you wrote a science-fiction story, how could you use cosmic noise in the story?" or "If you write a blog entry about a cosmic joke in someone's life, what might the blog be about?" or "If you created a time line of cosmic time, what events would you put on it?"

2. **Modeling**: Write another set of model words on the board. Suggestions are *transport, portable, porter, export, deport,* and *transportation.* Have volunteers circle specific word parts, as directed. Then model finding the meanings of prefixes, suffixes, and roots in print and/or digital dictionaries. Demonstrate how to insert a hyphen after a prefix (e.g., *ex-*) and before a suffix (e.g., *-er*) to look up a word part. Demonstrate that some common phrases may be found in dictionaries (e.g., cosmic dust, cosmic noise).

3. **Shared Practice**: Pass out copies of the handout, and group students in pairs. Have each pair complete items 1–3 on the handout.

   Note: You can break the lesson here, continuing on another day.

4. **Wrap-Up**: For homework or independent in-class work, have each student complete items 4–6 on the handout.

Differentiation

For students who need extra support

- Create and display posters of common prefixes, suffixes, and roots, and their meanings. Review the posters during the introduction to this lesson. As students read and write for other classes, continually refer to the posters, linking the word parts to words in the students' texts.

For advanced students

- Have students keep logs of words and word parts for a week; then meet one-on-one or in small groups to review the logs. Allow volunteers to teach one word to the class.

Assessment

Score the handout by awarding 4 points to each chart cell completed correctly. This means that each word-chart is worth a total of 16 points except for "3. Photography," which has five cells and is worth 20 points. A top score is 100.

Additional Resources

- Charts of prefixes, suffixes, roots, and their meanings are readily available on Internet sites. For example, Scholastic has charts of the most common prefixes and suffixes along with meanings and keywords: teacher.scholastic.com/reading/bestpractices/vocabulary/pdf/prefixes_suffixes.pdf.

- Funbrain has an interactive multiple-choice game to help students learn word roots: www.funbrain.com/roots/index.html.

Notes

After implementing the lesson, make notes on what worked and what you would change next time.

_____

_____

_____

_____

Word Parts Activity Sheet

For each word, use a dictionary to find out information about each word part and whole word. Then write a sentence to answer the question.

1. Autograph

word root:	prefix:
root's meaning:	prefix's meaning:
word's definition:	
Write a sentence about a time you signed your autograph.	

2. Photograph

word root:	prefix:
root's meaning:	prefix's meaning:
word's definition:	

If you could have your photograph taken with anybody, alive or dead, who would it be? Write a sentence to express your answer.

3. Photography

word root:	prefix:	suffix:
root's meaning:	prefix's meaning:	suffix's meaning:
word's definition:		
Write a sentence about a time you saw interesting photography.		

4. Graphic

word root:	suffix:
root's meaning:	suffix's meaning:
word's definition:	
Write a sentence to tell what kind of graphic feature you could use to help explain where the fire exits are in your school.	

5. Telegraph

word root:	prefix:
root's meaning:	prefix's meaning:
word's definition:	
Write a sentence to tell why someone might send a telegraph.	

6. Graphology

word root:	suffix:
root's meaning:	suffix's meaning:
word's definition:	
If you signed up for a workshop on graphology, what would you study? Write a sentence to express your answer.	

Easy As Pie!

Similes and Metaphors

Grade Levels: 4–5

Time Frame: Approximately one or two class periods

Overview: Beginning in grade 4, the Common Core State Standards ask students to begin learning to identify and interpret different types of figurative language. This lesson focuses on similes and metaphors.

Common Core State Standards

- 4: Language, Standard 5: Demonstrate understanding of figurative language, word relationships, and nuances in word meanings. a. Explain the meaning of simple similes and metaphors (e.g., *as pretty as a picture*) in context.

- 5: Language, Standard 5: Demonstrate understanding of figurative language, word relationships, and nuances in word meanings. a. Interpret figurative language, including similes and metaphors, in context.

Objectives

- Students will learn to identify and interpret similes and metaphors in the context of a sentence or paragraph.

Background Knowledge Required

No particular background knowledge is required for this lesson.

Materials Needed

- Copies of the poem "Flint," by Christina Rossetti, available at library.thinkquest.org/ J0112392/simileclassics.html

- Copies of the handout: Simile and Metaphor Activity Sheet, p. 200

Agenda

1. **Introduce Simile**: On the board, draw a few simple sketches of items that are related by concept or theme. For example, using the concept of weight, draw and label a feather, a brick, and a boulder. Ask students how they might use the word *feather* to describe a puppy. How might they use the word *brick* to describe a sandwich? How might they use the word *boulder* to describe a book bag? As students work to create descriptions, guide them to create similes—for example, light as a feather, solid as a brick, heavy as a boulder. Write out at least one simile per sketch. Explain that a

simile is a type of figurative language. It compares two things by using a word such as *like* or *as.* Ask students how similes might help people understand an idea or imagine an object. For example, how does comparing a sandwich to a brick help you to imagine how it feels in your stomach? Similes also make sentences more interesting. For example, which is more interesting: "My book bag is heavy" or "My book bag feels like a boulder hanging from my shoulders"?

2. **Full-Class Activity**: Ask students to follow along on their copies as you read "Flint" aloud. Taking the first three lines one at a time, guide students in identifying and explaining the simile in each line. Which word of comparison does each line use? (All three lines use *as.*) Ask students how they might rewrite each line to use the word *like* instead of *as?*

3. **Introduce Metaphor**: Go back to the sketches on the board. Remind students that a simile is one type of comparison. Another type is the metaphor. A metaphor compares two things by using a form of the verb *to be*—in other words, a metaphor says that one thing *is* the other thing. To demonstrate, rephrase each of the similes as a metaphor. Examples are these: This puppy is a feather. The sandwich was a brick in my stomach. This book bag is a boulder on my shoulder. Write the metaphors underneath the similes to help with comparison. Ask volunteers to use the three sketches (or new ones that you create) to inspire additional metaphors.

   Note: To split this lesson into two days, you can stop at this point. Before picking up with item 4 below, review some of the similes and metaphors you created in steps 1–3. You can use some of the differentiation activities listed later in this lesson plan to round out a day's lesson.

4. **Small-Group Activity**: Organize students into small groups and ask them to complete part 1 of the handout (items 1–4).

5. **Wrap-Up**: As a full class, go over part 1 of the handout. Different groups can share their explanations of the similes and metaphors. As you discuss each one, ask students to identify whether it is a simile or metaphor. How do they know? (A simile uses *like* or *as.* A metaphor says that one thing *is* the other thing.) If you have time, ask volunteers to suggest an additional simile or metaphor to use in a sentence to extend each paragraph.

6. **Homework or Independent In-Class Work**: Have students complete part 2 of the handout (items 5–9).

Differentiation

For students who need extra support

- On a poster, display a list of simple similes and a separate list of simple metaphors. In each simile or metaphor, underline the key word (*like, as, is,* or *was*). Review the charts before asking small groups to complete the handout.

- Create a simple fill-in-the-blank worksheet to help students create similes. For instance, "_____ as a mouse" or "_____ as a firecracker." To help students master metaphors, ask each student to decide which animal he or she is most like. They should write two sentences: one that uses a metaphor to express which animal they are and one that explains the metaphor. For instance, "Alex is a dolphin. He is friendly and playful."

For advanced students

- Ask volunteers to help you extend the simile and metaphor charts. As you explain the activity in the second bulleted item above, ask volunteers to give examples of answers. They might enjoy using family members as the subjects of these sentences.

Assessment

Evaluate students' work on part 1 of the handout to make sure they understand how to identify and explain similes and metaphors. To assign a grade, you can use a 10-point scale, awarding 1 point for each correct identification of a simile or metaphor and 1 point for each logical explanation.

Additional Resources

- You can find lists of common similes and their meanings by using *list of similes* as an Internet search term. One search result is this page from My English Club: www.englishclub.com/vocabulary/figures-similes-list.htm.

- This page from My English Club gives a few examples of simple metaphors: www .englishclub.com/vocabulary/figures-metaphor.htm. It goes on to give examples of implied metaphors, which are more complex than what the Common Core expects elementary-school students to learn.

Notes

After implementing the lesson, make notes on what worked and what you would change next time.

_____

_____

_____

_____

Simile and Metaphor Activity Sheet

Part 1: Read each paragraph. Find the simile or metaphor and underline it. Then write an explanation of what the simile or metaphor means.

> Every morning at my house, we eat breakfast at the crack of dawn. My mom likes to cook big breakfasts. The scrambled eggs are a mountain on the platter. The pancakes are fluffy and sweet. I soak them in strawberry syrup. With food like this, who wouldn't want to get up early?

1. What does the simile or metaphor mean? _____

_____

> Kaylee was happy when her family adopted a kitten. She promised that she would give the kitten food and water every day. Dad told Kaylee that there was one thing she needed to do before anything else. She needed to name the kitten! Kaylee petted the kitten. Its fur was soft as cotton. "I'll name him Cottonball," Kaylee said.

2. What does the simile or metaphor mean? _____

_____

In art class, Devon's teacher said that they would make valentines for their friends. Devon looked at the paper heart lying on his desk. What could he write on the valentine? Finally, he grabbed a pen and wrote, "Roses are red. Violets are blue. You are my sunshine, and I like you!"

3. What does the simile or metaphor mean? _____

_____

The room was dark, and the smell of sugar filled the air. Ten people crouched in the darkness. They were as quiet as mice. Then they heard the sound of the door creaking open. The overhead light came on. Everyone jumped up and yelled, "Surprise! Happy birthday!"

4. What does the simile or metaphor mean? _____

_____

Part 2: Read each paragraph. Find the simile or metaphor and underline it. Then, write an explanation of what the simile or metaphor means.

I have a dog named Tinkerbell. She weighs only 5 pounds, but she is as fierce as a lion. When someone rings the doorbell, she barks loudly. If I roll a mini-tennis ball across the floor, she chases it down and bites it. She has taught me that even the smallest person can be brave.

5. What does the simile or metaphor mean? _____

_____

At summer camp, a group of us sat around the campfire. It sparked and flickered in the center of a ring of rocks. In the firelight, my best friend's eyes were shiny stars. We roasted marshmallows on sticks and then smashed them with chocolate between graham crackers. Yum!

6. What does the simile or metaphor mean? _____

_____

One of the highlights of my summer is the farmer's market. I don't care about the vegetables. What I care about are the snow cones and the kettle corn! After eating a cold treat, my lips are as cold as ice. I give my mom a big kiss on the cheek, and she laughs and pushes me away in fun.

7. What does the simile or metaphor mean? _____

_____

Heavy raindrops were drumbeats on the roof. Lightning lit up the sky in sudden flashes, quickly followed by the boom of thunder. I wished I could stay snug in my bed, but there was just one problem. I was certain that a ghost had floated past my open bedroom door. I gathered my courage to go investigate.

8. What does the simile or metaphor mean? _____

_____

Jake and Lily rode their dirt bikes up the side of a rocky hill. It was slow going, but the effort was worth it. Now came the fun part: speeding down the hill! As they sped over rocks and clumps of grass, their bikes bounced wildly. The kids' laughter rang out like bells.

9. What does the simile or metaphor mean? _____

_____

Selecting Rich, Complex Texts for Student Reading

Grades K–5

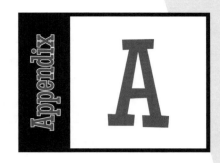

A variety of resources are available in your search for rich, complex texts for student reading. A few top-notch resources are the following:

- **American Library Association.** Find lists of children's book and media award winners on the ALA website under Book, Print, and Media Awards. In the menu at the left, select the subcategory Children and Young Adults. Examples are the Theodor Seuss Geisel Award, Coretta Scott King Book Award, Notable Children's Books, Notable Children's Recordings, Great Web Sites for Kids, Caldecott Medal winners, and Newbery Medal winners. Go to www.ala.org/awardsgrants/awards/browse/bpma?showfilter=no.

- **Appendix B of the Common Core Standards for English Language Arts & Literacy in History/Social Studies, Science, and Technical Subjects.** This appendix lists nearly 150 exemplar texts grouped by genre and includes excerpts of each. They are divided into grade bands (K–1, 2–3, 4–5). Go to www.corestandards.org/assets/Appendix_B.pdf. *Note: These lists are merely suggestions and are in no way a mandatory or exclusive list of texts. Teachers should feel confident in choosing sources other than these exemplar texts.*

- **Association for Library Service to Children.** The ALSC maintains lists of notable books and media for children. Go to www.ala.org/alsc/awardsgrants.

- *Children and Libraries* is the journal of the Association for Library Services to Children. Browse it for recommendation-packed articles on specific genres. For example, in volume 4, no. 3 (summer/fall 2006, pages 35–41), Sylvia M. Vardell contributes "A Place for Poetry." The article discusses 13 poems, giving suggestions for how to read them aloud and how to develop kid-friendly activities using the poem. A sidebar lists 12 additional poems.

- *Children's Core Collection.* Ask a local librarian if you can peruse the library's copy of H. W. Wilson Publishing Company's *Children's Core Collection*. This resource annotates and evaluates fiction (including graphic novels), nonfiction (including technology, social sciences and sciences), story collections, picture books and magazines for preschool through sixth grade. *Note: The word* Core *in the title does not refer to the Common Core.*

- **EBSCO*host*.** Check to see if your school or public library subscribes to this searchable database. It includes full-text articles from magazines and newspapers as well as e-books and audio books. To learn more about the kid-friendly interface and the lists of possibilities, go to http://ebscohost.com/us-elementary-schools.

- **The Horn Book.** *The Horn Book Magazine* has short reviews (some starred) of current picture books, fiction, poetry and song, nonfiction, and audio books, with each review noting one or two reading levels: primary, intermediate, middle school, or high school. *The Horn Book Guide* is a semi-annual publication (print and online) that rates and reviews titles published in the previous six months, indexed for ease of use. Go to http:// www.hbook.com.

- **The Junior Library Guild** creates lists of outstanding books, national- and state-award winners, and themes (e.g., summer reading, women's history) for grades pre-k through 6. While the lists are aimed at librarians who want to expand their collections, they are equally useful to teachers. Go to http://www.juniorlibraryguild.com/awards/?p=awards.

- **Lexile Framework for Reading.** To get lists of books that are leveled at grade level (or just below or just above), you can go to www.lexile.com, type in the grade you teach, choose book topics, and click Submit. You can sort for a wide range of topics, including biography, social issues, science and technology, graphic novels, animals, nature, fairy tales, and more. You can also type in the title of a book in the Quick Book Search box to find out its Lexile measure. For example, *Charlotte's Web* is 680L, which corresponds to a grade 3 or higher reading level.

- **Librarians.** Children's and youth librarians are usually enthusiastic about compiling lists of quality texts for teachers, given sufficient lead time. You might request nonfiction texts at a specific reading level, for example, or an assortment of fiction and nonfiction on a topic such as the solar system. You might need books or articles with maps, charts, diagrams, and timelines. Even if you don't need an entire reading list, librarians (who spend hours reading reviews of books in catalogs and journals) are happy to help you identify reputable texts that will serve your teaching purpose.

- **Scholastic News Magazines.** Scholastic publishes classroom magazines leveled to student readers and correlated to Common Core standards. The texts increase in difficulty as the year progresses. *Let's Find Out!*, *Scholastic News*, *Storyworks*, and *SuperScience* are a few examples. Depending on the magazine, the texts are informational or a variety of text types and may include charts, graphs, maps, and links to online videos. Go to http:// classroommagazines.scholastic.com to see all the magazines; look for the link to Common Core information.

- *School Library Journal.* Ask a school librarian if you can peruse a few copies of this monthly journal. The year-end Best Books issue is helpful. In any issue, flip to "The Book Review," a section of reviews of fiction and nonfiction. Look for starred reviews in the subsection for Preschool to Grade 4. For example, in the January 2008 issue, a starred review of Cathryn Falwell's *Scoot!* gives examples of "[s]trong, predictable rhymes" that "bounce across the pages" and "[u]nusual, lively words" that "extend vocabulary" (page 86). The book is recommended for preschool through grade 2. Special review sections focus on themes (such as black history) in picture books. In the December 2008 issue, Joyce Adams Burner's "Legends and Unsung Heroes" reviews websites, CDs, DVDs, and picture books on topics such as Heroic Biographies and the Civil Rights Movement (pages 54–59).

Sample Opinion Writing Prompts

Grades K–5

While acknowledging the importance of informative and narrative writing, the Common Core introduces a new emphasis on opinion writing in grades K–5. The following writing prompts, organized by grade level, are intended to provide ideas and inspiration as you incorporate opinion writing into your curriculum.

Feel free to modify these samples as needed to fit your teaching purposes. With many of these prompts, you can adapt them to the grade above or below the one listed by adding or removing specific criteria in a grade's writing standard. The opinion-writing standards are included in full, for easy reference.

To create your own prompts, keep this tip in mind: Build the writing task around a subjective word or phrase such as *best, worst, favorite,* or *most [insert adjective].* You can create quick writing tasks by having students write (or draw) for three or five minutes in response to a prompt such as "What is your favorite toy (or book or whatever)? Why is it your favorite?" These quick tasks let students focus on forming an opinion and giving a reason or two. In contrast, the longer writing tasks that follow require students to produce more sophisticated written responses.

Kindergarten students:

Use a combination of drawing, dictating, and writing to compose opinion pieces in which they tell a reader the topic or the name of the book they are writing about and state an opinion or preference about the topic or book (e.g., *My favorite book is . . .*).

(Writing Standard 1)

Kindergarten

These writing tasks are meant to be read aloud to the students.

As students learn to write words and sentences, modify the writing tasks to include writing their ideas in words or sentences and then reading them to the teacher or another adult.

Writing Prompt 1

Context for Writing: Read aloud a picture storybook to the class. Choose a story that focuses on one or two main human or animal characters. Display the book (or write its title on the board) while students work on the writing task.

Writing Task: Which character in the story did you like best? Draw a picture of your favorite character. Draw details to show why this character is your favorite. Think about what you want to say. Then, tell your teacher why this is your favorite character. Remember to tell the title of the story.

Writing Prompt 2

Context for Writing: Read aloud an informational science book to the class. Suggested topics are butterflies, frogs, the rainforest, volcanoes, weather, and the seasons. Display the book (or write its title on the board) while students work on the writing task.

Writing Task: What is the most interesting thing you learned from the book? Draw a picture of the most interesting thing in the book. Draw details to show why it is interesting. Think about what you want to say. Then, tell your teacher why this is the most interesting thing in the book. Remember to tell the title of the book.

Writing Prompt 3

Context for Writing: Read aloud a funny story. Any of the George and Martha stories by James Marshall should work well; non-series stories or picture storybooks will also work well. Display the book (or write the story's title on the board) while students work on the writing task.

Writing Task: What was the funniest part of the story? Why did it make you laugh? Draw a picture to show the funniest part of the story. Draw details to show what made you laugh. Think about what you want to say. Then, tell your teacher why this is the funniest part of the story. Remember to tell the title of the book.

Writing Prompt 4

Context for Writing: Read aloud three silly nursery rhymes. Write each title on the board, along with a picture cue. For example, draw an egg on top of a stone wall as a picture cue to "Humpty Dumpty."

Writing Task: Which rhyme is the silliest? Why is it the silliest? Draw a picture to show why the rhyme is silly. Think about what you want to say. Then, tell your teacher why this rhyme is the silliest. Remember to tell the title of the rhyme.

Writing Prompt 5

Context for Writing: Read aloud a nonfiction book about a world culture other than the United States. Display the book (or write its title on the board) while students work on the writing task.

Writing Task: Would you want to visit the place in the book? Why would you want to go there, or why would you *not* want to go there? Draw a picture to show why you would or would not want to go to this place. Draw details to show what you like or don't like about this place. Think about what you want to say. Then, tell your teacher why you want to visit this place, or why you don't want to visit. Remember to tell the title of the book.

Variation: Ask students to draw two pictures: one to show what they liked about the place, and the other to show what they didn't like about the place. Alter the writing task to include telling or writing details to support each drawing.

> ## Grade 1 students:
>
> Write opinion pieces in which they introduce the topic or name the book they are writing about, state an opinion, supply a reason for the opinion, and provide some sense of closure.
>
> (Writing Standard 1)

Grade 1

The writing tasks below are meant to be read aloud by a teacher who then guides students through each numbered step in the process. You might also write a simplified version of the steps on the board for students to read, using just a keyword or two. For example, in Writing Prompt 1, the first three steps would be "Picture," "Title," and "Decision."

Later in the year, consider having students read a text independently. Discuss the text as a class, and then guide them through the steps of the writing task.

Later in the year, decrease the use of the repetitive "Write a sentence that . . ." part of each writing step. Instead, use a direct verb such as *tell* or *explain*, allowing students to write one or more sentences per numbered step.

As students build their skill of giving supporting details, examples, or reasons, ask them to give more than one supporting reason. Writing Prompt 5, for example, asks for two reasons.

Writing Prompt 1

Context for Writing: Read aloud a short narrative book. One of the Step into Reading books about Arthur, such as *Arthur Lost in the Museum* by Marc Brown, would work well.

Writing Task: Characters in books make decisions about what to do, just like real people. Think about the story. What is one thing that the character decided to do? Was this a good decision or a bad decision? Now write some sentences about the book. Here is what to do:

1. Draw a picture about the character and what he or she did.

2. Write a sentence that tells the title of the book.

3. Write a sentence that tells what decision the character made.

4. Was this a good decision or bad decision? Write a sentence that tells what you think.

5. Why was this a good decision or bad decision? Write a sentence to tell why.

6. Should other people make the same decision? Write a sentence that tells what you think.

Writing Prompt 2

Context for Writing: Read aloud an informational text on a topic such as healthy foods, sports, manners, or friendship.

Writing Task: Some books give good advice. What good advice did this book give? Write some sentences to tell about the good advice. Here is what to do:

1. Draw a picture about the good advice. (For example, if the good advice is to eat fruit, draw fruit.)

2. Write a sentence that tells what this book is about.

3. Write a sentence that tells one thing people should do. Tell about something in the book.

4. Why should people do this? Write a sentence to tell why.

5. Do you think people will be glad they did this thing? Write a sentence to tell what you think.

Writing Prompt 3

Context for Writing: If your school has a mascot, discuss the mascot and what it stands for. For example, an eagle might stand for freedom; a tiger might stand for bravery. If your school does not have a mascot, introduce the concept and talk about different kinds of mascots and what they stand for. Explain that schools have mascots to bring good luck and to remind students to pay attention to what the mascot stands for.

Writing Task: If our class could have a mascot, what should it be? Write some sentences to tell what you think. Here is what to do:

1. Draw a picture of the mascot that you chose.

2. Write a sentence that tells what a mascot is.

3. Write a sentence that tells what the class mascot should be.

4. Write a sentence that tells what the mascot stands for.

5. Why is this a good choice for a mascot? Write a sentence to tell why it is a good choice.

Writing Prompt 4

Context for Writing: Read a nonfiction text about a biome such as a desert, a forest, a wetland, or a tundra. You don't need to use the word *biome*; instead, focus on details that help define the type of region.

Writing Task: What is the most important thing that people should know about [insert name of biome]? Write a few sentences to tell why people should know this. Here is what to do:

1. Draw a picture about the [insert name of biome].

2. Write a sentence that tells what a [insert name of biome] is.

3. Write a sentence to tell the most important thing people should know about this place.

4. Why is this important to know? Write a sentence to tell why.

5. Write a sentence to tell whether or not kids would enjoy learning more about this place.

Writing Prompt 5

Context for Writing: Ask students to tell you about characters in books they have read. Tell them that they will write about their favorite character and tell why this is their favorite.

Writing Task: Different people like different characters best. What is your favorite character in a book? Write about why this character is your favorite. Here is what to do:

1. Draw a picture about your favorite character. Put in details to show why this is your favorite.

2. Write a sentence to tell who your favorite character is.

3. Write a sentence to tell one reason why this character is your favorite. Give a detail to help make your reason clear. For example, if the character is funny, what is something funny that he did or said?

4. Write a sentence to tell *another* reason why this character is your favorite. Give a detail to help make your reason clear.

5. Write a sentence to tell who would like to read about this character (girls? boys? first-graders?).

Grade 2 students:

Write opinion pieces in which they introduce the topic or book they are writing about, state an opinion, supply reasons that support the opinion, use linking words (e.g., *because, and, also*) to connect opinions and reasons, and provide a concluding statement or section.

(Writing Standard 1)

Grade 2

These prompts are meant to be read aloud to the class. At first, you may need to guide students through each bulleted step in the writing process. Later in the year, students should be able to reread the prompts on their own as they work on their drafts.

As students gain skill in explaining two reasons to support an opinion, challenge them to include three reasons—just make sure the text is complex enough to support three reasons.

Writing Prompt 1

Context for Writing: Use this prompt after students have read a narrative with strong human or animal characters.

Writing Task: Write an opinion about a character in the story.

- Tell which character is your favorite.

- Give a reason why he or she is your favorite. Then, tell about a detail from the story to make your reason clear. *Tip:* Use the word *because* to link ideas together.

- Give another reason why he or she is your favorite. Give a detail from the story to make your reason clear. *Tip:* Use the word *and* or *also* to link ideas together.

- Do you think your friends would like to read the story? Write one or two sentences to answer this question.

- Write a title for the paper you wrote.

Writing Prompt 2

Context for Writing: Use this prompt after reading aloud, or having students read, two informational books on the same topic. Choose a how-to or self-help topic such as how to play a sport, be a good friend, draw an animal, or plant a seed or garden. You can help students prepare to write this opinion paper by having them complete a Venn diagram or T-chart to compare the two books.

Writing Task: Write an opinion about the books that you read.

- Tell which book was more helpful to you.

- Give a reason why this book was more helpful. Then, give an example from the book to make your reason clear. *Tip:* Use the word *because* to link ideas together.

- Give another reason why this book was more helpful. *Tip:* Use the word *another* or *also* to add the reason. Then give an example from the book to make your reason clear.

- Will you use ideas from this book in real life? Write one or two sentences to answer this question.

- Write a title for the paper you wrote.

Writing Prompt 3

Context for Writing: Use this prompt after reading several legends or myths.

Writing Task: Write an opinion about what makes someone a hero.

- Give the name of the character you are writing about.

- Give the title of the story he or she is in.

- Tell what makes this character a hero. Use details from the story to make your ideas clear. *Tip:* Use the word *because* to connect ideas.

- Why should other kids read this story? Write one or two sentences to answer this question.

- Write a title for your paper.

Writing Prompt 4

Context for Writing: Before using this prompt, have a full-class discussion about treating others with respect. What does that word mean? What are examples of respect? Of disrespect? Why should classmates and schoolmates treat one another with respect? What can happen if they don't?

Writing Task: Write an opinion about respect at your school (or in your class).

- What does the word *respect* mean?

- Do you think kids at your school mostly show respect to others? Or do they not show respect? Write sentences to tell what you think.

- Give details to make your opinion clear. Give examples of what kids have done or said. For this paper, use made-up names for the people you write about. *Tip:* Use the word *and* or *also* to connect ideas.

- Are you happy or unhappy with the level of respect at your school?

- Write a title for your paper.

Writing Prompt 5

Context for Writing: Use this prompt after reading short biographies or encyclopedia entries about several early U.S. presidents, such as Washington, Jefferson, and Lincoln.

Writing Task: Write an opinion about a United States president.

- Tell which president you think helped our country the most.

- Give **two** reasons why you think he helped the most. Give a fact about the president to explain each reason. *Tip:* Use the word *because* or *since* to link ideas.

- Do you think this president would be a good role model for our nation's president today? Write one or two sentences to answer this question.

- Write a title for your opinion paper.

Grade 3 students:

Write opinion pieces on topics or texts, supporting a point of view with reasons.

a. Introduce the topic or text they are writing about, state an opinion, and create an organizational structure that lists reasons.

b. Provide reasons that support the opinion.

c. Use linking words and phrases (e.g., *because, therefore, since, for example*) to connect opinions and reasons.

d. Provide a concluding statement or section.

(Writing Standard 1)

Grade 3

These prompts are meant to be read aloud while students follow along and ask for any necessary clarification. Then, students should be able to reread the prompts independently as they work on their drafts.

Writing Prompt 1

Context for Writing: Use this prompt after students have read a mystery narrative. Any book in the A to Z Mysteries series by Ron Roy will work well. Suspenseful stories are an alternative to mysteries; just revise the writing task to ask whether students think the story kept them in suspense (wondering with curiosity what would happen next), or not.

Writing Task: Write an opinion paper about a mystery story.

- Tell the title and the author of the story.

- Did you think the mystery was easy or hard to solve? Write one or more sentences to answer this question.

- Give **three** examples from the book to show why the mystery was easy or hard to solve. *Tip:* Give the best example first. Give the next-best example after that. Give the third-best example last.

- Tell what kind of reader would enjoy reading this mystery story. *Tip:* Use the word *because* to connect ideas.

- Write a title at the top of your paper.

Writing Prompt 2

Context for Writing: Use this prompt after reading about several traditions from around the world. Examples are holiday or birthday traditions, customs surrounding special events (such as losing a tooth or bringing home a new baby), or family traditions.

Writing Task: Write an opinion paper about a tradition that the United States should have.

- Explain what a tradition is.

- What is a tradition that the United States *should* have, but doesn't have? Give details about the tradition. *Tip:* Use words such as *also* and *another* to add more details.

- Give **two** reasons why you think the United States should have this tradition. *Tip:* Use words such as *therefore* and *because* to link ideas.

- What kind of person in the United States would agree with your opinion about adding this tradition? Write a few sentences to explain who would agree with you.

- Write a title at the top of your paper.

Writing Prompt 3

Context for Writing: Use this prompt after reading about two or more kinds of nocturnal animals such as bats, owls, mice, hedgehogs, fireflies, and cats. Text types might include magazine articles, encyclopedia articles, or informational picture books.

Writing Task: Write an opinion paper about the most interesting night creature.

- What is a night creature? Begin your paper by giving this information. Give examples of two or more kinds of night creatures.

- Tell which animal you think is most interesting.

- Give **three** reasons why it is interesting. Explain each reason by giving facts or details about the animal. Use details from the book or article you read. *Tip:* Put your reasons in order so that you give the best reason last. This will help keep your reader interested in what you have to say.

- Write an ending for your paper. A good ending might do one of these things: 1) Tell where to find out more information about the animal. 2) Quickly list the reasons that you wrote about and say again how interesting this animal is. 3) Tell what kind of person is sure to find this animal interesting.

- Write a title at the top of your paper.

Writing Prompt 4

Context for Writing: Use this prompt after reading a story, drama, or poem. The prompt uses the key words *most exciting,* but you can substitute phrasing such as *most interesting, most beautiful, funniest, silliest, saddest, most surprising,* and so on.

Writing Task: Write an opinion paper about the most exciting part of the work that you read.

- Give the title of the work and the name of the author.

- Tell what the work is about.

- Tell what is the most exciting part of the work. *Tip:* Use correct words, such as *chapter, paragraph, act, scene, stanza,* or *line.*

- Give **two** reasons why you think this is the most exciting part. Give details or examples from the work to make your reasons clear. *Tip:* Use phrases such as *for example* to connect ideas.

- Write an ending for your paper. A good ending might do one of these things: 1) Suggest that people read and enjoy the work for themselves. 2) Tell what kind of person is sure to enjoy reading the work.

- Write a title at the top of your paper.

Writing Prompt 5

Context for Writing: Use this prompt after reading a book in the You Wouldn't Want To series, such as *You Wouldn't Want to Be an American Colonist* by Jacqueline Morley. Help students see that the title of the book expresses an opinion.

Writing Task: Write a paper to tell whether or not you agree with the author's opinion.

- Give the title of the book and the name of the author.

- Tell what the author's opinion is.

- Tell whether or not you agree with the author's opinion.

- Give **three** reasons why you do or don't agree with the author's opinion. Give a detail or example from the book to support each reason. *Tip:* Use words such as *because* and *for example* to link ideas.

- Write an ending for your paper. A good ending might re-tell your opinion about the author's opinion. It might ask people to read the book for themselves so they can form their own opinion.

- Write a title at the top of your paper.

Grade 4 students:

Write opinion pieces on topics or texts, supporting a point of view with reasons and information.

a. Introduce a topic or text clearly, state an opinion, and create an organizational structure in which related ideas are grouped to support the writer's purpose.

b. Provide reasons that are supported by facts and details.

c. Link opinions and reasons using words and phrases (e.g., *for instance, in order to, in addition*).

d. Provide a concluding statement or section related to the opinion presented.

(Writing Standard 1)

Grade 4

As with previous grades, these prompts are meant to be read aloud and explained. Then, students should be able to reread the prompts independently as they work on their drafts.

Writing Prompt 1

Context for Writing: Use this prompt after reading several short informational texts about inventions (or one longer text that covers multiple inventions).

Writing Task: Write an opinion paper about inventions. What is the most important invention you read about?

- Introduce the topic of inventions. Name some important inventions.

- Give your opinion. Which invention in the list you gave is the most important?

- Why is this invention the most important? Give reasons to support your opinion. Support each reason with a fact or example from the text. *Tip:* Use linking words to organize ideas. Examples are *first, second, in addition,* and *another.*

- Bring the paper to a close. You can do this by re-telling your opinion. Another idea is to quickly retell why this invention is the most important.

- Be sure to give your paper an interesting title!

Writing Prompt 2

Context for Writing: Use this prompt after students have read a story or drama and then examined a visual or oral presentation of the text. For longer works, such as *Tuck Everlasting* by Natalie Babbitt, you might choose one chapter or scene to work with. For shorter works, such as a version of "Little Red Riding Hood," you could first read a picture storybook aloud without showing the pictures, and then read the book again while showing the pictures.

Writing Task: Write an opinion paper about the two versions of the story: the version that you read (or listened to), and the version that you saw. Which version does a better job of telling the story?

- Introduce the story you are writing about by giving its title. Tell who wrote the version you read. Tell something about the second version. Is it a film? A story told in pictures?

- Give your opinion. Which version of the story does a better job of telling the story?

- How does one version do a better job? Give reasons to support your opinion. Support each reason with a detail or example from a version of the story. *Tip:* Use linking words and phrases to connect ideas. Examples are *for instance* and *for example.*

- Give your reasons in a logical order. For example, start with the most obvious reason. Work up to the reason that is most surprising or interesting.

- Bring the paper to a close by re-telling your opinion.

- Be sure to give your paper an interesting title!

Writing Prompt 3

Context for Writing: Use this prompt in conjunction with a discussion of a moral lesson in a work of narrative fiction or narrative nonfiction (e.g., a biography). Make sure that students identify a moral lesson (e.g., it's better to be yourself than fail at trying to be someone else) as opposed to just a topic (e.g., being yourself).

Writing Task: Write an opinion paper about a moral lesson in the story you read. Do you agree or disagree with the moral of the story?

- Introduce the story you are writing about by giving its title and telling who wrote it.

- Tell what the moral of the story is.

- Give your opinion. Do you agree or disagree with the moral of the story?

- Why do you agree or disagree? Give reasons to support your opinion. Use details from the story to help explain your reasons. *Tip:* Link your opinion with a reason by using a word or phrase such as *because, for instance,* or *for example.*

- Form strong paragraphs by grouping related ideas together. For example, give one supporting reason and supporting details in one paragraph. Then, give the next reason and its supporting details in the next paragraph.

- Give the paper a strong ending. For example, you could restate your opinion or quickly list your reasons.

- Be sure to give your paper an interesting title!

Writing Prompt 4

Context for Writing: Use this prompt after reading about various types of severe storms or natural disasters. You could have small groups perform a shared research project to locate and bring in short texts about storms or disasters that you choose in advance.

Writing Task: Write an opinion paper about storms (or disasters). Which type do you think is the biggest threat where you live?

- Introduce the topic by telling what a severe storm (or natural disaster) is.

- Tell what kinds of storms (disasters) happen in your state or region. Be sure to name your state or region!

- Give your opinion. Which type of storm (disaster) is the biggest threat where you live?

- What makes this storm (disaster) the biggest threat? Give reasons to support your opinion. Use facts and examples from the text to make your reasons clear. *Tip:* Link your opinion with a reason by using a word or phrase such as *because, for instance,* or *for example.*

- Form strong paragraphs by grouping related ideas together. For example, in one paragraph, tell how the storm (disaster) threatens people. In another paragraph, tell how it threatens the environment.

- Give the paper a strong ending. For example, restate the main reason why this storm (disaster) is the type that is the biggest threat where you live.

- Be sure to give your paper an interesting title!

Writing Prompt 5

Context for Writing: Use this prompt after students compare and contrast a firsthand and secondhand account of the same historical event. (The event could be an event of national importance or an event in the life of a person such as Laura Ingalls Wilder or Ruby Bridges.)

Writing Task: Write an opinion paper about two texts that tell about the same event. Which text does a better job?

- Introduce the event. In a few sentences, sum up what happened.

- Give the titles and authors of the two texts you read.

- Give your opinion. Which text does a better job of telling what happened?

- How does this text do a better job? Give reasons to support your opinion. Use examples and details from the text to make your reasons clear. *Tip:* Use words and phrases such as *for instance* and *for example* to link reasons to supporting details.

- Arrange your paragraphs in a logical order. For example, give examples in chronological order (the order that they happened in real life). Or give your reasons in order from the least strong to the strongest.

- Give a concluding statement or paragraph. For example, tell why people who are interested in this topic would want to read this text.

- Be sure to give your paper an interesting title!

Grade 5 students:

Write opinion pieces on topics or texts, supporting a point of view with reasons and information.

   a. Introduce a topic or text clearly, state an opinion, and create an organizational structure in which ideas are logically grouped to support the writer's purpose.

   b. Provide logically ordered reasons that are supported by facts and details.

   c. Link opinion and reasons using words, phrases, and clauses (e.g., *consequently, specifically*).

   d. Provide a concluding statement or section related to the opinion presented.

(Writing Standard 1)

Grade 5

These prompts are meant to be read aloud and discussed, giving students a chance to ask questions. Then, students should be able to reread the prompts independently as they work on their papers.

   You can help students form and polish their opinions by conducting discussions (full-class or small-group) on the writing topic before assigning the writing task. You can shorten any of these assignments by asking for just one reason. You can adapt these to shared-writing projects by asking students to contribute one or two paragraphs to a group-written paper.

Writing Prompt 1

Context for Writing: Use this prompt in conjunction with a full-class discussion on the theme "room for improvement in our school." You might suggest topics such as nutrition, respect, fun, safety, cleanliness, or school spirit. You can extend this assignment by having students write a second opinion paper telling how the school or its students should make the necessary changes.

Writing Task: In your opinion, what part of your school most needs improvement? Write a paper to explain your opinion.

▪ Introduce your topic: room for improvement at your school. Then tell what most needs improvement.

▪ Give strong reasons to support your opinion. Support each reason with facts, details, and examples about your school.

▪ Use connectors to link ideas. Some examples are *first, next, more important, because of this problem,* and *specifically.* You can come up with other connectors, too.

▪ Give your paper a concluding sentence or paragraph. What is the main idea you want your readers to remember?

▪ Give your paper an interesting title!

Writing Prompt 2

Context for Writing: Use this prompt after students have read a short story, novel, or biography.

Writing Task: Think about what the main character did in the story. In your opinion, should the main character have done anything differently? Write a paper to explain your opinion.

- Introduce the title of the book you are writing about. Give the author's name.

- Introduce the character you are writing about. Give a few important details about him or her and identify the main problem the character faces.

- State your opinion about whether this character should have done anything differently.

- Give strong reasons to support your opinion. Support each reason with facts, details, and examples from the story. Use at least **one** direct quotation from the story.

- Link reasons to your opinion by using words such as *one reason, another reason*, and *the most important reason.*

- Give your paper a concluding sentence or paragraph. Help readers care about your opinion. For example, tell how the book would have been better if the character had done something differently. Or state that, as your reasons show, the character made the best decisions possible.

- Give your paper an interesting title!

Writing Prompt 3

Context for Writing: Use this prompt after reading an informational text (or multiple texts) on a geographical location such as your city or state, a national park, or a historical site such as a battleground. Make sure the text gives enough information about the place so students can pick and choose among reasons to visit.

Writing Task: In your opinion, what are the top three reasons to visit [insert name of place]? Write a paper to explain your opinion.

- Introduce the place you are writing about, and identify what kinds of people might want to visit.

- State your opinion about the top three reasons to visit this place.

- Explain each reason in the body of your paper. Give the reasons in a logical order. For example, you might arrange them from least to most important. You might arrange them in the order that visitors to the place would experience them.

- Support each reason with details and examples from the text you read. *Tip:* Use signal words such as *for instance* and *specifically* to introduce a detail or example.

- Give your paper a concluding sentence or paragraph. You might restate your opinion, for example. Or you might quickly list the top three reasons so that they stay in your readers' mind.

- Don't forget to give your paper an interesting title!

Writing Prompt 4

Context for Writing: Compile a list of four or five web pages created for kids. You can find safe pages on the FBI Kids Page, National Geographic Kids, Discovery Kids, Sports Illustrated Kids, and Ranger Rick, to name a few. Assign individual students or groups a specific page to evaluate, either "live" on the Web or via a printout you provide.

Writing Task: You have been asked to review a Web page. Would you recommend this page to other kids your age? Why or why not? Write a paper to explain your opinion of the page.

- In the paper's introduction, give the name of the website and the name of the page you are writing about. State whether or not you recommend the page to kids your age.

- In the body of the paper, give reasons to support your opinion. Support each reason with details and examples from the web page. Refer to specific parts of the web page. For example, give the titles of subsections or menus, or refer to icons or images.

- Group related ideas together. For example, you might write one paragraph about the web page's information, another paragraph on the page's graphics, and another page on the page's user-friendliness.

- In the paper's conclusion, restate your opinion, but use different words from those you used in the introduction. Since these are the last sentences your reader will read, you want them to make a lasting impression.

- Give your paper an interesting title!

Writing Prompt 5

Context for Writing: This prompt works well in conjunction with reading a poem or narrative that has multiple examples of figurative language. As students read the text, have them take notes on the author's use of figurative language.

Writing Task: Authors use figurative language to communicate ideas creatively and to create an effect on the reader. Think about the story (poem) that you read. In your opinion, does the figurative language make the work more appealing or less appealing to readers your age? Write a paper to explain your opinion.

- Introduce the topic of figurative language, the title of the work, and the author.

- State your opinion about the author's use of figurative language.

- Give **two or three** strong reasons to make your opinion clear and convincing. *Tip:* Use words such as *consequently* and *therefore* to link reasons to your opinion.

- Support each reason with details or examples from the text. Use at least **one** direct quotation from the text to support a reason.

- Give your paper a concluding sentence or paragraph. *Tip:* Use a phrase such as *for these reasons* or *as these reasons show* to introduce a restatement of your opinion.

- Don't forget to give your paper an interesting title!

Blank Lesson Plan Template

Use the following template to create your own Common Core lesson plans in reading, writing, speaking/listening, and language. Remember that your lessons should be integrated when possible and cover more than one standard.

Common Core Lesson Plan

Topic/Title: _____

Grade Level:

Time Frame:

Overview:

Common Core State Standards

-
-
-
-

Objectives

-
-
-
-

Background Knowledge Required

Materials Needed

-
-
-
-

Agenda

1.

2.

3.

4.

5.

Extend the Lesson

-
-

Differentiation

For students who need extra support

-
-

For advanced students

-
-

Assessment

-
-
-
-

Additional Resources

-
-

Notes

After implementing the lesson, reflect on what worked and what you would change the next time.

_____

_____

_____

_____

References

Arechiga, D. (2012). *Reaching English language learners in every classroom: Energizers for teaching and learning*. Larchmont, NY: Eye On Education.

Blackburn, B. R. (2012). *Rigor made easy: Getting started*. Larchmont, NY: Eye On Education.

Coleman, D., & Pimentel, S. (2012). *Revised publishers' criteria for the Common Core State Standards in English language arts and literacy, grades K–2*. Washington, DC: The National Association of State Boards of Education, Council of Chief State School Officers, Achieve, and the Council of the Great City Schools.

Morris, Lisa. (2012). *Awakening brilliance in the writer's workshop: Using notebooks, mentor texts, and the writing process*. Larchmont, NY: Eye On Education.

National Governors Association Center for Best Practices, Council of Chief State School Officers (2010). *Common Core State Standards for English language arts*. Washington, D.C.: National Governors Association Center for Best Practices, Council of Chief State School Officers.

Roberts, T., & Billings, L. (2012). *Teaching critical thinking: using seminars for 21st century literacy*. Larchmont, NY: Eye On Education.

Sulla, Nancy (2012). *Students taking charge: Inside the learner-active, technology-infused classroom*. Larchmont, NY: Eye On Education.